CULTOGRAPHIES

CULTOGRAPHIES is a new list of individual studies devoted to the analysis of cult film. The series provides a comprehensive introduction to those films which have attained the coveted status of a cult classic, focusing on their particular appeal, the ways in which they have been conceived, constructed and received, and their place in the broader popular cultural landscape. For more information, please visit www.cultographies.com

Series editors: Ernest Mathijs (University of British Columbia) and Jamie Sexton (Northumbria University)

OTHER PUBLISHED TITLES IN THE CULTOGRAPHIES SERIES

THE ROCKY HORROR PICTURE SHOW
Jeffrey Weinstock

DONNIE DARKO
Geoff King

THIS IS SPINAL TAP
Ethan de Seife

BAD TASTE
Jim Barratt

SUPERSTAR: THE KAREN CARPENTER STORY
Glyn Davis

THE EVIL DEAD
Kate Egan

BLADE RUNNER
Matt Hills

BRING ME THE HEAD OF ALFREDO GARCIA
Ian Cooper

FASTER, PUSSYCAT! KILL! KILL!
Dean DeFino

QUADROPHENIA
Stephen Glynn

FRANKENSTEIN

Robert Horton

WALLFLOWER PRESS
LONDON & NEW YORK

A Wallflower Press Book
Published by
Columbia University Press
Publishers Since 1893
New York • Chichester, West Sussex
cup.columbia.edu

A complete CIP record is available from the Library of Congress

ISBN 978-0-231-16743-7 (pbk. : alk. paper)
ISBN 978-0-231-85056-8 (e-book)

Book design by Elsa Mathern

Columbia University Press books are printed on permanent
and durable acid-free paper.
This book is printed on paper with recycled content.
Printed in the United States of America

p 10 9 8 7 6 5 4 3 2 1

CONTENTS

Acknowledgements   vii

1   Welcome to Nightmare Theatre:
Meeting *Frankenstein*   1

2   Assembling a Monster   13

3   The Monster Mash: Sons of the House
of Frankenstein   27

4   Beyond the Clouds and Stars:
Surveying *Frankenstein*   44

5   The Monster's Place   84

Appendix: The *Frankenstein* Family Tree   97

Bibliography   113
Index   117

Interviewer: He's one of the great images of the twentieth century, more important than the *Mona Lisa*!

James Whale: Oh, don't be daft. It's just make-up and padding and a big actor.

– *Gods and Monsters*

ACKNOWLEDGEMENTS

Anyone who writes a book becomes a Doctor Frankenstein, tinkering with parts and toiling to bring the creature to life. In this case, that process involved watching a lot of Frankensteinian spinoffs, most of which are not as awful as *Frankenstein Island*, but not as good as *Bride of Frankenstein*, either. Thus I owe my wife a debt of gratitude for sitting through many of these offerings, and am happy to dedicate the book to my dear monster, Evyan.

I would like to thank Stephanie Ogle, of Seattle's venerable Cinema Books, for pointing out to me that Wallflower Press was producing some intriguing lines of books on film. That's how I came to read about the 'Cultographies' series even before their first instalment had been published, and thought it would be a wonderful way to fulfil a lifelong ambition: to write a book-length study of a single film. Thanks to Ernest Mathijs for editorial support and to Jamie Sexton, Yoram Allon and the Wallflower/Columbia University Press people for allowing that *Frankenstein* might fit under the 'Cult Movie' banner in a sort of slantwise but interesting way. General thanks, too, to Tom Keogh, Kathleen Murphy, Richard T. Jameson, Mary Jane Knecht and Mark Rahner.

The opening chapter makes clear my debt to 'Nightmare Theatre' and the tradition of late-night horror movies on television, a tradition mostly gone, despite the occasional tongue-in-cheek attempt to revive it. So, revising the words of Dr. Septimus Pretorius: 'To an old world of gods and monsters!'

Robert Horton, February 2014

1

WELCOME TO NIGHTMARE THEATRE: MEETING *FRANKENSTEIN*

If a cult is anything, it has rituals and ceremonies and a schedule of worship. And here is ours: Friday nights, gathered in somebody's basement, sleeping bags staked out on the floor. There are chocolate-bar wrappers scattered around and a half-eaten bag of Fritos waiting to be finished off. This is 1970, or possibly 1971 or 1969, and as twelve-year-olds our beverage of choice is something innocuous, Kool-Aid or Coke. It's almost 11:30, so the parents have already looked down a final time and said their goodnights, and the lights are appropriately low. If anybody managed to smuggle in an issue of *Playboy* it's been put away, because we need to concentrate on television now. There's a plaster Madonna looming in a corner, that home icon of the Catholic family, which is apt because we are gathered here for something like a religious ceremony ourselves.

The local 11 o'clock news programme on KIRO-TV, Seattle's channel 7, is ending. As always, the broadcast signs off with an editorial comment from station manager Lloyd E. Cooney, a bespectacled square perpetually out of step with the turbulent era (channel 7, owned by the Mormon Church, is a conservative business). Strange, then, that every Friday night Cooney's bland homilies are immediately replaced by a dark dungeon, a fiend in a coffin and three hours of evil.

At 11:30 sharp comes 'Nightmare Theatre', a double feature of horror movies. Each film is introduced by channel 7's resident horror-movie host, known as 'The Count' (actually a station floor director named Joe Towey). His make-up is a Halloween-costume version of Dracula, with cape and fangs. He clambers out of a coffin, welcomes us, and introduces the first feature of the evening; his Bela Lugosi accent is terrible, but his maniacal laughter is accomplished.

Tonight it's that most famous title of all, *Frankenstein* (1931). The film is already legendary in my mind – I am well aware of its status in the horror pantheon. I have seen that green-faced, heavy-booted image in books and TV shows (though I am still somewhat confused about whether 'Frankenstein' is the name of the monster or the name of the mad scientist), and finally I am allowed to stay up late enough to watch the film on television. Here with other like-minded fifth-graders, I await the arrival of something monumental and, with luck, terrifying.

The Count finishes his intro with a cackle. When the film begins, it too has a host, a neat little grey man who comes out from behind a curtain and delivers a message that sounds both sinister and whimsical:

> Mr. Carl Laemmle feels it would be a little unkind to present this picture without just a word of friendly warning. We are about to unfold the story of Frankenstein, a man of science who sought to create a man after his own image without reckoning upon God. It is one of the strangest tales ever told. It deals with the two great mysteries of creation – Life and Death. I think it will thrill you.

2

Edward Van Sloan, conveying Mr. Carl Laemmle's warning as *Frankenstein* begins

It may shock you. It might even horrify you. So if any of you feel that you do not care to subject your nerves to such a strain, now is your chance to... Well... we've warned you...

This is going to be good.

And here it comes: a clammy graveyard (ah, excellent start), tasty stuff about an abnormal brain, sensational lab scene in an electrical storm. Now the entrance of the monster: first a tease, then the horrible face. Can I stand to look at it? Yes. It's weird but bearable. The Monster stomps and kills but also suffers, and the villagers go after him in a burning windmill. The End. The movie has delivered, and those of us in the room have lived through something. In childhood, staying up late to watch horror movies is a rite of passage, a test, a communal ceremony in which fears are met, endured, analysed. Nightmares will come, but that's part of the ritual too (although my fears at bedtime tend more toward the Wolf Man, whose dexterity and ferocious claws are more threatening than the Frankenstein monster's clomping brute strength). We have seen *Frankenstein*, and the Monster is ours – a hero, in a strange way.

I first saw *Frankenstein* almost forty years after it had been made, and by then it was firmly entrenched as a cult classic. (Can a movie that was an enormous box-office success and a permanent fixture in popular culture be called a cult film? I believe so, especially if we emphasise the religious overtones contained in the word 'cult'. And *Frankenstein* may have many fans all over the world, but there is still something forbidden about it, something outside the main of respectable culture.) Even though I was coming to the picture as part of a second, or perhaps third, generation of fans, even though I had already read about the Monster and seen his image refracted in everything from *Mad* magazine to *The Munsters*, it still seemed fresh – and thanks to the peculiar intimacy of late-night television, that first experience was also deeply personal. *Frankenstein* belongs in a dark room, late at night. The moviegoers of the 1930s and 1940s who saw the film in theatres are the people that gave the Monster its first life, without question. (Mel Brooks, who would make a detailed parody of the mythos in his 1974 comedy *Young Frankenstein*, amusingly recalls his boyhood fear that – against all logic – the Frankenstein monster would somehow stomp its way to Brooks's boyhood home in Brooklyn.) Yet it was the TV generation that turned the Monster and his ilk into icons, a generation crammed with future filmmakers weaned on late-night horror films (among them Steven Spielberg, Robert Zemeckis, Sam Raimi and Joe Dante).

What is it about *Frankenstein*, in particular, that seems to touch a nerve? Some of the issues are embedded in the celebrated book that inspired the film. Even if Hollywood jettisoned many of the Romantic complexities of Mary Shelley's novel, the book nevertheless manages to grin out from beneath the streamlining and backlot sets. At the elemental level, surely *Frankenstein* gets to us because it is a story of birth – and of 'giving birth'. The mystery of how we got here is one childhood draw. Another early childhood anxiety surrounds the realisation of death, and *Frankenstein* messes with the possibility of life after death; it even makes the process look scientific and achievable. How could children not be intrigued by the movie?

GLOW IN THE DARK

The warning delivered by Universal stock player Edward Van Sloan at the film's beginning, however fruity its language, does announce the stakes: this is a story of the great mysteries of creation – Life and Death. The movie explicitly invokes a Creator, comparing Man's power with that of God, notably in a famously censored line of dialogue after Henry Frankenstein's successful experiment, when the ecstatic scientist exclaims, 'Now I know what it feels like to be God!' The film, of course, will punish Frankenstein for his hubris, but one wonders whether the excitingly portrayed creation myth is the one that sticks with viewers, not the dutiful reminder about Man's reach exceeding his grasp.

Even in the pulp trappings of a Universal horror film, and even to a child (especially to a child), *Frankenstein* gives off the heady whiff of grandness, of something large at play. I think as a child I drew power from *Frankenstein*, the bigness of its reach, the bluntness of its argument. The Monster, a child like me, was still learning how to use his body, how to relate to his parent, how to live in a world that seems hostile; he was clumsy with social interaction (until *Bride of Frankenstein* [1935], hopeless with words), but capable of enormous strength. Yes, his raw, unfocused power was scary. But damned if you didn't end up rooting for him at the end. He was Mary Shelley's outcast, misunderstood, wandering in a hostile environment. The villagers with their torches, by contrast, looked like small-minded, ignorant rabble, quick to anger. Who wouldn't gravitate toward the Monster?

There were other levels of identification for my fifth-grade self. *Frankenstein* and movies like it were frowned on by parents, teachers, and just about everybody who occupied a position of power over the average twelve-year-old. The battles lines were drawn, and we were on the side of the monsters. A strong sense of association with something outlaw, something officially disdained by mainstream culture, is almost always part of the cult movie experience, and the cult model was at play in that basement in 1970: we were the believers, hungry for the feeling of community that a cult bestows upon the enthusiast. Let the Establishment have its *Sound of Music* (1965) and *Love Story* (1970) – next week 'Nightmare Theatre' is showing *The Curse of the Werewolf* (1961) and *Dementia 13* (1963).

As in any cult, our worship needed objects and relics and a deeper system of belief. I cherished a coffee-table book by Denis Gifford, *A Pictorial History of Horror Movies*, which gathered together grisly photographs of countless movies I'd never seen or heard of. Soon I would get a model kit to build my own Frankenstein Monster – an activity that actually puts the user in the position of Frankenstein himself, of assembling different parts to make a creature, although here the pieces came not from a graveyard but from a nearby hobby shop. I also had a card game, 'Monster Old Maid', adorned with the Universal monsters. (The 'old maid' was Dracula's daughter,

Cover of Aurora's first monster model, 'Glow in the Dark' version; cover art by James Bama

in a particularly toothy grimace.) The gathering of talismans is another aspect of cult worship, and posters or magazines devoted to the monsters were an important part of extending one's devotion. I laboured over the Aurora monster models and assembled most of the major characters: splashing nice red paint over the otherwise drab wrappings of the Mummy, painstakingly hanging the bats on the branches framing Dracula's come-hither pose. This was the phase when Aurora was offering their 'glow-in-the-dark' versions of the monster models, with the somewhat bizarre effect of an otherwise realistically-painted Wolf Man crowned by a pale, light-green head. But it did glow in the dark, at least for a while.

One might ask why an easily-frightened child would surround himself with these frightening images. (On the other hand, believers in Christianity favour the depiction of a man-god being tortured to death on a cross, so perhaps the leap for a Catholic schoolboy isn't that far.) Keeping the monsters close at hand is surely a way to manage them, and the fear they represent. Here is an external representation of a child's dread, kept near the bedside; when the child wakes up in the morning, it's one more tiny victory over the forces of fear.

But the game was not an individual one. My friends also collected those monster models, which we could compare and contrast, and the communal viewings of 'Nightmare Theatre' were an important part of maintaining the enthusiasm for the monsters. This was the era before man had dominance over movies; an individual could not own a movie (unless you were some kind of 16 mm collector), and movies could not be rented. It was a random thing, and you'd have to check the schedule to see if one of the Universal titans was going to be showing that week. One of the hallmarks of 'Nightmare Theatre', which pulled its stock from a collection of films licensed for broadcast, was the crapshoot nature of watching it. Yes, you might get a goodie such as *Bucket of Blood* (1959), or an atomic giant-bug picture. But sometimes the gods were stingy. The schedule might list a promising title (*The Man They Could Not Hang* [1939] or *The Frozen Ghost* [1945]) and a *bona fide* horror star (Lon Chaney, Jr. or Boris Karloff), but the movie would play and the horror never came. These were the sleep-inducers, the price you paid for discovering the gems.

Frankenstein was in the regular 'Nightmare Theatre' rotation and thus aired every six months or so, as did other Universal 1930s classics, later Universal non-classics like *The Thing*

That Couldn't Die (1958), dubbed Mexican horror, and Roger Corman cheapies. Because of the hodgepodge nature of the schedule, one could see (entirely out of logical order) all of the original Universal *Frankenstein* pictures along with entries from the Hammer Films *Frankenstein* run, as well as such *outré* items as the drive-in schlocker *I Was a Teenage Frankenstein* (1957) and the Japanese *Frankenstein Conquers the World* (1965). Those early *Frankenstein* viewings blend together with the film's sequels, which extended the story and increased the sense of a complicated mythos around the Monster.

This *Frankenstein* mythology had its constants, despite the wild variations in country of origin, time period, or quality. One constant was the name Frankenstein, a veritable 'open sesame' to all things horrific; the name was in the public domain, so anybody could take a crack at the concept. Universal copyrighted the classic make-up designed for Boris Karloff by Jack Pierce, an indelible image as familiar as the Coca-Cola logo – the flat-top skull and neck bolts, the distinctive black bangs. Yet those elements seemed to pop up everywhere, from cartoons (comic-strip and editorial) to advertisements; even the Monster stalking Japan in *Frankenstein Conquers the World* had the definitive Monster hairdo, like a piece of black Astroturf set outside a haunted house's sliding door. Frankenstein's Monster became a ritualised element, like a stock figure of Japanese drama. He might change his make-up, his geographical location, or his era, yet certain conventions would be in place; give a filmmaker a laboratory, some electric gizmos, and perhaps an abnormal brain, and he's got himself a Frankenstein picture.

Every child wants order over chaos, and these elements provide a comforting sense of unity. The intricately-knit realm of horror films inculcates a notion of cinema as a world, a comprehensible universe. For children, the horror film is a seductive *entrée* to an idea of cinema because it creates a world that, while frightening, has rules. These rules (garlic, silver bullet, full moon) amount to a belief system, and this system applies not merely to individual films but the entire galaxy of horror pictures. There's the sense of the cinema as an interlocking pattern of conventions and tropes, which can be compared across the spectrum of sequels and remakes (thus the busy chatter on horror movie website message boards, where the cultish details of horror – the good, bad, and obscure – can be parsed by like-minded enthusiasts).

For me that sense was enhanced by the recurrence of certain actors, most prominently Boris Karloff and Bela Lugosi – even their exotic names sounded the gong of fear. The modern horror world was presided over by the likes of Vincent Price and Peter Cushing, who were almost as fine in their undertaker-like bearing. But lesser players, too, could be relied on to scurry from film to film: Edward Van Sloan, the fusspot vampire hunter from *Dracula* (1931), provided avuncular ballast to *Frankenstein* and *The Mummy* (1932) as well. Dwight Frye, an unfortunate lackey in *Dracula* and *Frankenstein*, would pop up in tiny parts in other shards of the Universal universe. Lon Chaney, Jr., Lionel Atwill, George Zucco, John Carradine…these people were as indestructible as the monsters. They became as familiar as relatives at holiday gatherings, or the faces of the martyrs in the book of saints.

This sense of an ordered universe is one of the lures, and the dangers, of cinema, and certainly those who fail to rise to the chaos of reality do so at risk of arrested development. But such childhood influences can remain as useful touchstones. Film scholar David Bordwell called the idea 'The Law of the Adolescent Window':

The cultural pastimes that attract us then, the ones we find ourselves drawn to and even obsessive about, will always have a powerful hold. We may broaden our tastes as we grow out of those years – we should, any-how – but the sports, hobbies, books, TV, movies, and music that we loved then we will always love…. Make no apologies. It's not mere nostalgia or guilty pleasure to revisit these creations. You can return to them as to old friends. Encountering them again, you remember when you took it for granted that anything was possible in your life. Their sharp, shining lines fitted your range of vision, and mostly they still do. (Bordwell 2007)

A key phrase there is 'We may broaden our tastes', which a certain number of cultists never quite get around to doing. The enthusiasm for cult movies can be a trap, when the taste for Underground culture, or 'termite art', as Manny Farber dubbed it, leads to a tunnel-vision loyalty to a genre or even a particular franchise – as witness the endless arcana of *Star Wars* devotees. But in its right place, Bordwell's 'Adolescent Window' becomes a mirror, and the well-past-adolescent cultist might look back and find his image there. In some ways writing this book is exactly that exercise for me: a way of returning to a cherished childhood idiom and learning how it lives for me today.

So, back to 'Nightmare Theatre': along with his mummies and mutants, The Count delivered a batch of films explor-ing the Frankenstein family tree. Its branches stretched far. There are cult movies that are stand-alone experiences; indeed the idea of a cult movie implies a smallish, specia-lised appeal, but *Frankenstein* is a fountainhead, a web, an industry. Its central figure literally would not die. The mon-ster perishes at the end of *Frankenstein* but is miraculously discovered alive at the beginning of *Bride of Frankenstein*, thus setting a pattern of death and resurrection that would continue through the other *Frankenstein* sequels and count-less horror pictures thereafter.

And here we come to a central issue in the child's response to *Frankenstein*. Belief systems generally invent an afterlife, or reincarnation, and so does this one: the Monster keeps returning, even after his many deaths, to go about his usual business. The cinema itself is a defiance of death, a graveyard where viewers can re-live past experiences, hear the voices of the dead, see people long gone. The Frankenstein Monster is the perfect leading man for this ritual. 'We belong dead,' he says of himself and his similarly hand-made mate in *Bride of Frankenstein*, but almost eight decades of film history argue otherwise.

2

ASSEMBLING A MONSTER

Jack Pierce had created unnerving make-up at Universal Pictures before, notably a tooth-baring, permanently grinning face for Conrad Veidt in *The Man Who Laughs* (1928). But this was on another level. Pierce worked for three weeks to develop the different pieces of face and body for this new project, about a manmade creature, with the patient collaboration of the actor – a little-known minor player in his early forties. Pierce applied cotton and collodion to build up the actor's brow, created an alarming flat skull-ridge to suggest drastic cranial surgery, and glued two electrodes at the sides of the neck, an inspired electrical touch that set the creation in the realm of science rather than magic. The fingernails and the skin beneath the eyes were blackened, and the actor's own physiognomy – the cheeks that sank into the face, beyond even the powers of the sculpting make-up – added to the sepulchral effect. Pierce surveyed the monstrosity sitting in the make-up chair before him and had an instinct. He shared it with the actor, whose name was Boris Karloff. 'This is going to be a big thing,' Pierce said.

It was an understatement. Pierce, with input from the film's director, James Whale, and a handful of studio artists, had created a visual icon that would outlast all of them. The year was 1931 and the film was *Frankenstein*, a property that would big-footedly lumber into pop-culture glory.

Of course 1931 was not the beginning of the *Frankenstein* project. When Pierce stared into Karloff's clay-like face, he was looking at an idea that had been born more than a hundred years earlier, during a celebrated literary idyll on the shores of Lake Geneva. Mary Wollstonecraft Godwin had conceived *Frankenstein* in the summer of 1816 – and the language of birth is appropriate here, because the novel is about birth, failed fatherhood, abandoned progeny. (The subject was close to Mary Godwin. Her mother had died ten days after Mary's birth, and Mary had recently given birth to her own second child, having lost the first in infancy.) During a stormy night at Villa Diodati near Geneva, in the company of her lover and future husband, the already-famous poet Percy Shelley, and the even more famous poet Lord Byron, the writerly party decided to challenge each other to concoct a ghost story. (This, in a way, is the first 'cult' of *Frankenstein*: like-minded enthusiasts, reading macabre tales to each other, hotly discussing art and science.) Shelley and Byron did not finish their efforts, although Byron's young doctor, John Polidori, eventually completed something of a Gothic classic, *The Vampyre*. Mary was inspired by the conversations, and by a terrible nightmare she endured, of unholy rebirth:

> I saw the pale student of unhallowed arts kneeling beside the thing he had put together. I saw the hideous phantasm of a man stretched out, and then, on the working of some powerful engine, show signs of life and stir with an uneasy, half-vital motion. (Shelley 1981: xxv)

Recalling the dream, she described the re-animator's horror at his loosed creation, thus also predicting the effect of her story on subsequent readers and movie-watchers:

He sleeps; but he is awakened; he opens his eyes; behold, the horrid thing stands at his bedside, opening his curtains and looking on him with yellow, watery, but speculative eyes. (1981: xxv)

Her story of a man who gives life to dead flesh, *Frankenstein, or, The Modern Prometheus*, was published anonymously in 1818. Despite or because of its lurid subject, it became popular and was almost immediately adapted for the stage; countless variations would follow. It is commonplace to describe the 1931 film of *Frankenstein* as a radical pruning of the novel, a Hollywood simplification of a complex work. This is true to a point; certainly the story-within-a-story structure is gone (the book is a group of letters from a sea captain named Walton to his sister, recounting a story told by Victor Frankenstein, a man picked up by Walton's ship in the arctic ice), and the book's geographical roaming is narrowed: the movie is set within Universal's idea of a Mittel-European village and environs, with little hint of the rich Romantic landscapes of Shelley's novel, the sublime sights that stir both Frankenstein and his creation (and to which the frozen Arctic framing sequences provide such a deadened, bleached counterpoint).

Much of this pruning had been anticipated by the stage versions, yet some of the novel's basic power comes through. The film's final shape was a process almost as complicated as Frankenstein's stitching of limbs and organs, showing the influence of a typical Hollywood string of baton-passers: playwrights, producers, screenwriters, directors, actors and, of course, Jack Pierce's putty and greasepaint. The movie was built upon countless iterations of Shelley's novel on stage; though they were not in the book, the conventions of the scientist's hapless assistant and a mob of angry villagers were already well-worn theatrical conventions.

Frankenstein had been made into a film before: in 1910, in a fascinating 13-minute version from the Thomas Edison Company; as a 1915 feature called *Life Without Soul*; and again in Italy in 1920 as *Il Mostro di Frankenstein*. But the roots of what would become Universal's classic were in a specific stage adaptation, written by Peggy Webling for the veteran barnstormer Hamilton Deane, an actor who had already scored with a touring show of *Dracula*. Webling's *Frankenstein: An Adventure in the Macabre* premiered in 1927, eventually reaching London's West End in 1930. Rewritten by John L. Balderston with the idea of staging it in the US, the property was bought for the movies by Universal's Carl Laemmle, Jr., the 22-year-old president of the company (and son of its founder). Laemmle's gamble on a screen version of *Dracula* had just paid off, and *Frankenstein* was envisioned as a vehicle for that film's star, Bela Lugosi.

On April 25, 1931, *Filmograph* announced that George Melford, who had directed the supple Spanish-language version of *Dracula* (1931), would direct *Frankenstein*. Before long French-born Robert Florey, who had made a kind of avant-garde classic with *The Life and Death of 9413, a Hollywood Extra* (1928), was assigned to the project, and set to work on the script. Florey and Lugosi shot a make-up test on the *Dracula* soundstage in June 1931, with Lugosi in some sort of monster get-up (accounts vary as to the nature of Lugosi's disfigurement). The test is lost, although Lugosi is widely reported to have been miffed at the idea of playing a wordless creature buried beneath prosthetics and a fright wig.

A *New York Times* piece of June 14, essentially an interview with Junior Laemmle, still trumpets Lugosi as 'the man-made monster,' with Karl Freund supposedly photographing the film. Laemmle was already playing coy about the material, which led the reporter to surmise, 'It has various startling effects that must remain secret until such time as they are permitted to burst on the public eye from the screen' (1931a: X4). However, the Lugosi-Florey *Frankenstein* would not enter film history; the project was abruptly handed over to another director. Florey and Lugosi immediately moved to an adaptation of Edgar Allan Poe's *Murders in the Rue Morgue* (1932), a slow but amazingly lurid horror picture with a script partly written by John Huston. The new director was an Englishman with a brief *résumé* in film.

THE STRONGEST MEAT

Frankenstein would now be directed by James Whale. And Whale would become the presiding spirit over *Frankenstein*, even if many writers contributed to the screenplay. Some of the carry-overs from adaptation to adaptation are fascinating: it was Peggy Webling, for instance, who swapped the first names of the novel's protagonist Victor Frankenstein and his best friend Henry Clerval, a seemingly irrelevant change that stuck in the film. Balderston added pyrotechnics to the trans-formation sequence; Mrs. Shelley had left the details of this out of her book. Florey and screenwriter Garrett Fort added a sequence in a burning windmill, which would become an es-sential part of *Frankenstein* lore. And one of the screenwrit-ers, Francis Faragoh or John Russell, contributed the twist of an 'abnormal brain' being used for the monster, a small detail that nevertheless affects the movie's theme – see Chapter 4 for more on that subject.

James Whale, born in 1889 in Dudley, Worcestershire, had come to Hollywood on the wings of his stage success, *Journey's End*, a World War I play by R.C. Sherriff. Whale was a curious contradiction, an elegant dandy originally from a poor mining town, a veteran of the war and former POW, a homosexual whose orientation was, by most accounts, not especially hidden. Whale's film of *Journey's End* was released in 1930, the same year as Universal's Oscar-winning blockbuster, *All Quiet on the Western Front*, and although Whale's film was overshadowed by the latter's success, Universal took notice. After making *Waterloo Bridge* (1931) for Laemmle, he was given his choice from a list of projects, and said he opted for *Frankenstein* because 'it was the strongest meat and gave me a chance to dabble in the macabre' (*New York Times* 1931e: X4).

To play the tightly-wound Henry Frankenstein, Whale tapped his leading man from *Journey's End* (play and film), Colin Clive. The actor, a descendant of 'Clive of India', had just the right screen presence for the obsessive role: doomy of mien and perpetually pitched on the verge of a nervous breakdown. Whale told the *New York Times* he had chosen Clive for his tenacity on screen, but also for a 'romantic quality which makes strong men leave civilization to shoot big game' (1931e: X4). Mae Clarke, another recent Whale collaborator, was chosen for the female lead; she had given a fresh, touching performance as the London prostitute surprised by the love of a soldier in *Waterloo Bridge*. *Dracula* being such a current success, two players from that film were brought over: Edward Van Sloan, *Dracula*'s vampire-hunter Van Helsing, and Dwight Frye, the vampire's deranged, insect-gobbling assistant. John Boles – tall, dark, and dull – would play Victor, the best friend. Whale brought Frederick Kerr, a dab hand with comic geezers (he had expertly essayed the soldier's blathering father in *Waterloo Bridge*), to play Baron Frankenstein.

Without Lugosi, who either rejected the part as beneath him or was not favoured by Whale, the production needed a creature. Whale's lover, the producer David Lewis, noticed Boris Karloff and recommended him to the director, who approached Karloff at the Universal commissary. That meeting has become the stuff of Hollywood legend, akin to Lana Turner being discovered on a stool at Schwab's Drugstore, and the encounter itself must have been more prosaic than Boris Karloff would later tell it. But you cannot blame Karloff: it was the lightning-bolt moment in his career, the meeting that changed his probable fate from that of a striking character actor to headlining cult icon.

Of course the name was invented – not by a studio hack but by the actor himself; he said Karloff was a family name on his mother's side, and Boris was a random inspiration. Born William Henry Pratt in 1887, youngest son of a family of respectable London diplomats, he was infected with the acting bug and set out for Canada as a young man. Years of trouping, and then a series of small parts and odd jobs, surely added to the lined, haunted look that would make his fame. In 1931 he was forty-four years old, had made over 70 movies, and was long past the point of a big break.

Whale summoned Karloff over to his table at the commissary, and said, 'Your face has startling possibilities.' The phrase sounds like a pick-up line, and perhaps Whale understood that directing actors was partly a matter of seduction. But flattery was needed, for then he would have to tell Karloff what kind of role this was. 'For the first time in my life,' Karloff said later, 'I had been gainfully employed long enough to buy myself some new clothes and spruce up a bit – actually, I rather fancied meself! Now, to hide all this new-found beauty under monster-makeup?' (Lindsay 1975: 54). But he took the job.

Karloff endured brutal sessions in Jack Pierce's make-up chair; after early tests, Karloff himself suggested that, as the monster looked not quite dead enough, he should have putty on his eyelids, weighing them down in a comatose gaze. (Karloff also had a bridge in his teeth that could be removed, which helped the hollows in his face grow deeper.) In a story perhaps burnished by legend, Karloff later said he knew they had clinched the monster when he wore his make-up on a stroll down a studio corridor and scared the wits out of an unsuspecting prop man. As it happened, Karloff was forced to eat lunch by himself during shooting, either because other commissary diners would have been turned off their food (see F. Scott Fitzgerald's story *Crazy Sunday* [1932] for a tale of just such a Hollywood meal) or because it was good publicity for the picture.

Whale brought his own strong design sense to the project, and could sketch on paper his ideas for sets and costumes. (Elsa Lanchester, who played both Mary Shelley and the monster's mate in *Bride of Frankenstein*, said that Whale demanded specific requirements for her Shelley dress, 'with iridescent, sequined butterflies and moons and stars,' even though the camera might not pick up such finery.) He was one of the many filmmakers awed by the influential 1920 German Expressionist film *The Cabinet of Dr. Caligari*, and he was a fan of the work of Paul Leni, who had been a set designer for Max Reinhardt's theatre in Berlin before becoming a film director himself. Leni, imported by the elder Laemmle to work at Universal, had already made a mark in the spookshow business with *The Cat and the Canary* (1927) and *The Man Who Laughs*, and was rumored to be the likely director for *Dracula* when he died in 1929, at age 44, from a tooth abscess that went untreated. According to Whale biographer James Curtis, Whale's experiences in a World War I prison of war camp in Holzminden had instilled in him a hatred for Germans, so perhaps Whale's linkage of horror with an overbearing Teutonic style comes from something other than just watching the great German movies of the 1920s.

In a note he wrote to Colin Clive before production began, Whale described his approach. 'There are none of Dracula's maniacal cackles,' he wrote. 'I want the picture to be a very modern, materialistic treatment of this medieval story – something of *Doctor Caligari*, something of Edgar Allan Poe, and of course a good deal of us' (*New York Times* 1931c: X5). That 'good deal of us' intrigues, suggesting Whale's awareness of the personal nature of his filmmaking (and perhaps a nod to the Frankensteinian relationship between directors and actors).

The production began shooting on August 24, 1931, with Colin Clive and Dwight Frye scuttling around a soundstage cemetery, looking to rob a grave. It wrapped on October 3, five days over schedule and slightly over budget at $291,000 (Weaver et al 2007: 43). The creation scene alone took five days to film; Whale felt it was the key sequence in the picture, 'because if the audience did not believe the thing had been really made, they would not be bothered with what it was supposed to do afterward' (*New York Times* 1931: X4). (Note calling the Monster 'it' rather than 'he'.) Whale, art director Charles Hall, and set designer Herman Rosse created a vertiginous laboratory set, in which Frankenstein's lifeless creation could be raised to the heights of the castle roof and zapped into animation by a passing lightning storm. The snapping Tesla coils and sputtering electrical gizmos of the lab were the creation of Kenneth Strickfaden, an electricity buff.

The two gentle Englishmen, Karloff and Whale, collaborated closely on the conception of the Monster, who they both viewed as a blameless, childlike creature. Whale would act out the gestures of the Monster, and the actor would apply his own soulful aura and expressive hands to the task. They differed on one sequence, a soon-to-be notorious scene in which the Monster meets a little girl called Maria at the side of the lake. Innocently following the girl's lead in tossing flowers in the lake, he hoists her in the air and heaves her in the water, where she vanishes. Karloff and other members of the crew objected to the fatal toss; he felt the monster would set Maria gently down on the surface of the water, but Whale insisted on the more violent action (Mank 1981: 32). Karloff later said that Whale justified the killing by saying, 'It's all part of the *ritual*.'

That intriguing phrase suggests Whale's awareness of the myth underlying the story, the sense that there were certain ceremonies that needed to be acted out along the way.

The child actress, Marilyn Harris, had to do two takes of the dunking, having failed to properly sink the first time through. Whale said she could have anything she wanted if she would do it again, and the kid asked for a dozen hard-boiled eggs. Whale came through with two dozen. (Her stepmother was irritated at the child for claiming such a modest prize.)

Karloff's daughter later said the actor suffered back problems from the rigours of his costume (the boots had lifts and extra weight, perhaps as much as 13 pounds per shoe) and from having to drag Colin Clive around the windmill set (Lindsay 1975: 56). Universal must have sensed something about Karloff's impact, for they cannily withheld his name from the opening credits of the film (some theatrical productions of *Frankenstein* had done similar tricks), replacing it with a question mark. Universal's movies ended with a credit roll cheerily headed by the words 'A Good Cast is Worth Repeating', and his name did appear at the end, but only as 'Karloff' – a mysterious touch with a whiff of the carnival sideshow.

Despite this, it did not occur to anyone at Universal to invite Karloff to the first screening of the picture, at Santa Barbara's Granada Theater, on October 29, 1931. The audience was terrified. Part of the *Frankenstein* legend – which ought to be true, even if it is apocryphal – is that the theatre's manager was awakened by telephone calls throughout the night from distraught patrons, who declared that if they could not sleep, neither would he (Jensen 1996: 27).

Universal then made the radical decision to change the ending. Originally, Henry Frankenstein was killed, along with the monster, in a fire in a windmill. Colin Clive, interviewed in November just before he sailed back to England after finishing the picture, spoke of how unusual it was for the main character to be killed off, 'as the producers generally prefer that the play end happily with the hero and the heroine clasped in each other's arms' (*New York Times* 1931d: X6). Sure enough, the producers felt that way again. Now Frankenstein would survive, to be reunited with Elizabeth. However, Colin Clive was already on an ocean liner halfway across the Atlantic, so a postscript scene was hastily added, with Frederick Kerr's Baron toasting the new union and declaring 'Here's to a son to the house of Frankenstein' (thereby predicting the titles of *two* future Universal sequels).

One other bit was needed. As the movie was clearly going to shock audiences, Laemmle Jr. and a slightly nervous Universal decided to add a spoken prologue, warning the audience in advance of the horrors to come. Edward Van Sloan, out of character, emerges from behind a curtain to speak to the imagined audience on behalf of 'Mr. Carl Laemmle', noting that the main character in the film pursued science 'without reckoning upon God.' Thus did Universal cover their bets with Catholic authorities who had expressed concerns about Frankenstein's hubristic bent. But the puckish, winking quality of the introduction (drafted by a team that included John Huston and Richard Schayer) clearly invites the audience to join in the nasty fun to come. It is an early model (perfected decades later by schlockmeister William Castle) of a movie campaign that provides audience titillation in the guise of a sober warning.

NATURALLY A MORBID AFFAIR

Publicity gimmicks were already a part of Hollywood's marketing machine, and the release of *Frankenstein* brought an assortment of shameless examples: ambulances sent to movie theatres, medical equipment kept at the ready, and frequent press releases about women fainting in theatres. A theatre manager in Chicago hired an actor to walk the streets dressed in a monster costume, prompting at least one more fainting spell.

The film might not have needed the gimmickry. If *Dracula* had shocked audiences, *Frankenstein* was even grislier. Even after its release, some changes would have to be made to the film Whale had shot, and the scene with the little girl by the lake was a prime target. For US consumption the sequence was shortened and its ending removed, so that it now left off before the Monster picked up Maria and threw her in the lake. This robbed the Monster of a significant character beat – his response to her sinking is not malevolence, but abjectness – and it actually made the implications of Maria's lifeless body in a subsequent scene more disturbing. Cuts were made to the film in different parts of the US, depending on state standards; in Britain, censors barred the discovery of Fritz's corpse and shortened the scene of the Monster stalking Elizabeth in her bridal chamber. (The end of the Maria scene, a key part of *Frankenstein* lore for many years, was restored to prints of the film in the mid-1980s.)

Lines of dialogue were also tampered with, although these were mostly excised for a late 1930s re-release. Most notoriously, Henry Frankenstein's ecstatic reaction after his creation has stirred for the first time – 'I know what it feels like to be God' – was deleted and covered over with a crack of thunder. Those lines would only be returned to the film during the age of home video.

While the movie was forcing American and Canadian censors to reach for their scissors in individual cities, it galvanised a chaotic censorship crisis going on in Britain. The British Board of Film Censors was under intense pressure to create a new rating, H, for Horror (the complicated alternative would be running each film past various boards of local censors), a controversy that was peaking just as *Frankenstein* came roaring in from its box-office triumph in the States. The Tivoli Theatre, where *Frankenstein* opened in London on January 25, 1932, posted a line in its advertisements that read, 'In Our Opinion, This Film is Unsuitable for Children', in an attempt to warn off unsuspecting parents and curious kiddies (Johnson 1997: 40). As 1932 wore on and the tide of horror pictures continued, the BBFC officially added the 'H' rating. (Some films were not even that lucky – *Freaks* (1932) was banned in the UK for thirty years.)

In the event, the film was banned in parts of Australia and Czechoslovakia, and drastically cut in most markets, including Germany, which approved the film only after an elaborate series of cuts and re-submissions to the censorship board. Such censorship problems became themselves a publicity tool, creating an aura of the forbidden, a sense of the movie as a dangerous 'test' that must be survived – a lure that continues in the horror film's appeal as a rite-of-passage shared experience.

Reviewers were frightened, but many were impressed. For the *New York Times*, Mordaunt Hall took a thoughtful stance, not at all glib or lofty: 'It is naturally a morbid, gruesome affair, but it is something to keep the spectator awake, for during its most spine-chilling periods it exacts attention... No matter what one may say about the melodramatic ideas here, there is no denying that it is far and away the most effective thing of its kind. Beside it *Dracula* is tame' (Hall 1931: 21). With some insight to the nature of nervous laughter, Hall observed that the movie 'aroused so much excitement at the Mayfair yesterday that many in the audience laughed to cover their true feelings'.

The *Times* of London was not as captivated. The reviewer admitted the transformation scene was 'ingenious and striking' but felt that the story, and Whale's interest in it, fell off badly after that. The *Sunday Times* called it 'the most sensational motion picture ever made'. A reviewer for *Film Weekly* clucked, 'It has no theme and points no moral. It is the kind of film which could only induce nightmares.' But in general the UK critics were intrigued, with the prevailing opinion perhaps best expressed by the *Daily Telegraph*: 'A good scream and a faint never did anyone any harm.'

Frankenstein was a box-office hit, striking a chord with audiences mired in the Great Depression. Irene Thirer, writing in the *New York Daily News*, said, 'We needed a weird, shadowy, spooky picture', as though acknowledging the dark temper of the times (Hitchcock 2007: 161). Reports of audience members fainting were probably trumped up by Universal's gleeful publicity machine, although in Cedar Rapids, Iowa, the fire department was called when a crowd got unruly trying to get into the theatre showing *Frankenstein*. There is no doubt the film landed with a shock. *Dracula* had been a drawing-room thriller with a sexy villain in a tuxedo, a suave Count who left behind discreet puncture marks in his victims' necks...even if he occasionally turned into a bat. *Frankenstein* was a hideous monster who did nasty things to children and brides.

The film rolled up huge profits, and the stage was set for an onslaught of monsters, a blooming of darkness on the silver screen. But Frankenstein's Monster himself was dead, burned and buried in rubble in a windmill. As it turned out, this was not a death, but a beginning.

3

THE MONSTER MASH:
SONS OF THE HOUSE OF FRANKENSTEIN

'I do think it a shame, Mary, to end your story quite so
suddenly.'

Prologue, *Bride of Frankenstein*

The triumph over death, the reversal of mortality – this idea
is at the heart of Mary Shelley's (and James Whale's, and
everybody else's) *Frankenstein*. If Victor Frankenstein could
restore life, why couldn't the movies?

The Monster dies at the end of the 1931 *Frankenstein*.
We see him fall in the burning windmill, we see the celebration of the survivors at the end. His re-appearance in *Bride
of Frankenstein*, released in 1935, can be chalked up to the
cynical needs of Universal Pictures, which knew a cash cow
when it saw one. Right?

On one level, of course the greedy boardroom numbers-
crunchers would want to duplicate a box-office success. But
the Monster's miraculous revival is also a wish of the audience, a collective refusal to let him die. Just as Frankenstein

restored his collection of organs and dead flesh to life, so the audience willed its Monster to return. The Monster is confused, abandoned and touchingly moved by the sight of sunlight. He did not ask to be born any more than any of the rest of us did. And we would not let him die.

In the gap between the November 1931 opening of *Frankenstein* and the April 1935 opening of *Bride of Frankenstein*, a raft of horror pictures entered the market, trying to capture the audience created by *Dracula* and *Frankenstein*. Florey and Lugosi had their consolation prize for losing *Frankenstein*, *Murders in the Rue Morgue*, and Whale and Karloff went to work on the hugely amusing *The Old Dark House* (1932), less a horror picture than a wry send-up of *Cat and the Canary*-style mysteries. Paramount had its *Dr. Jekyll and Mr. Hyde* (1931) in theatres at the same time *Frankenstein* arrived, but upped the revulsion factor with *Island of Lost Souls* (1932), a take on the H.G. Wells novel *The Island of Dr. Moreau*, with Charles Laughton as the physician-creep and Lugosi as a human/animal experiment. Lugosi also graced *White Zombie* (1932), directed by Victor Halperin, a genuinely eerie number about the undead in Haiti. Warner Bros. came through with *Mystery of the Wax Museum* (1933), a film that owes as much to the wisecracking-reporter tradition as it does to the horror picture. MGM, the Rolls-Royce of studios, amazingly allowed Tod Browning to make *Freaks*, that dark eruption of sideshow strangeness.

Karloff's instant popularity put him hard to work; to add to his new mystique, he was sometimes billed only by his last name. Anointed as the successor to 'Man of a Thousand Faces' Lon Chaney, Karloff assumed a variety of make-up challenges, including *The Mask of Fu Manchu* and *The Mummy* (both 1932). He was teamed with Lugosi in Edgar G. Ulmer's evocative *The Black Cat* (1934), a film that explicitly tied the new depravity onscreen to the hangover from the real-life horrors of the First World War. (David J. Skal's superbly researched 'cultural history of horror', *The Monster Show*, persuasively argues that this boom in horror had its roots in the war, roots fed by the Great Depression.)

And so the ripple effect from Universal's twin horror lords was immediate, but it would also be long-lived. *Frankenstein* had already proved its durability, of course, being over a hundred years old by the time Universal got its hands on the property; the name 'Frankenstein' had long been in currency as shorthand for all manner of man-made disasters. (In the *New York Times* of Oct. 25, 1931 – less than a month before the movie opened – an advertisement for a new book, *Frankenstein Incorporated*, by I. Maurice Wormser, proclaimed that 'Modern Society is a Frankenstein which has created a new monster – the corporation of overwhelming size and unrestrained power', and promised an analysis of 'the abuses which threaten our business structure and have done much to bring about the present crisis' (1931f: BR12) The term 'Frankenstein', freely used to refer to either the creator of something bad or the uncontrollable creation, was in fact ubiquitous.

But if Frankenstein (or *Frankenstein*, or 'Frankenstein', or whatever we are talking about) already had a profile, the 1931 film would begin an entirely new international cult following. And if a cult arranges itself around a single film, it nourishes itself even more from the array of sequels and remakes that follow, and in that sense *Frankenstein* is the prototype of a modern cinematic phenomenon, one that bursts the boundaries of the frame into different media, a cosmos unto itself. It is fitting then that the first sequel, and the confirmation of the monster's reproducibility as a pop-culture deity, should be at the hands of James Whale and Boris Karloff again.

Along with *The Old Dark House*, Whale had also made *The Invisible Man* (1933), a clever adaptation of the H.G.

Wells novel (and surely his most 'British' film, full of fog over moors, Cockney biddy Una O'Connor and jet-black humour). Whale had pronounced himself not interested in *The Return of Frankenstein*, as the sequel was initially called, claiming to have 'squeezed the idea dry' (Hitchcock, 2007: 172) with the first film. Karloff was game, but now feeling protective of the Monster – he was sceptical about having the Monster speak in the sequel, and when Universal came up with a lighter, cork-filled pair of boots to stomp around in, Karloff stuck with the heavy originals, to keep that Monster feel. Universal, naturally, stirred the publicity fires, including the announcement that Karloff would wear a veil over his head while moving between dressing room and soundstage. (Yes, his make-up had already been seen in the first film, but a few new burn marks had been added, and make-up wizard Jack Pierce had singed some of his hair away – as one writer described it, 'All the fetching bangs and lovelocks of the synthetic man are gone' [*New York Times*, 1935: X3]).

Re-titled *Bride of Frankenstein* with Whale back at the helm, the project used elements from the Shelley novel (where an attempt to create a bride for the monster is derailed) and even the person of Mrs. Shelley herself. A prologue takes us to the Villa Diodati, where Lord Byron and Percy Shelley tease the coquettish Mary about how such a sweet-faced woman could write such a fearful novel as *Frankenstein*. Here is confirmation of the gathering cult: the *Frankenstein* franchise has already gone 'meta', commenting on itself as a phenomenon. In fact, at this moment the universe of *Frankenstein* really begins to expand into the colossus it would soon become. The central metaphor of the novel and movie – that having been given life, the creation goes beyond the control of its creator – now took shape in the franchise itself. (Graham Greene, then reviewing films, saw it all coming with some measure of disapproval; he was not a fan. At the release of *Bride of Frankenstein*, he recognised that Mary Shelley's nightmare had become an industry: 'It rolls on indefinitely, the first dream and the first elaboration of it in her novel *Frankenstein*, gathering silliness and solemnity as it goes; presently, I have no doubt, it will be colour-shot and televised; later in the Brave New World [Aldous Huxley's novel had just come out] to become a smelly' [1993: 5].)

Greene's demurral notwithstanding, *Bride of Frankenstein* was quite well-reviewed upon its release; London's *Daily Herald* gushed, '[I]t is wonderful!' and the *Sunday Times* pronounced Karloff 'colossally fine'. Frank S. Nugent, in the *New York Times*, deemed it 'a first-rate horror film' and keenly added, 'The Monster should become an institution, like Charlie Chan'. The *Times* of London was more sceptical, insisting, 'It is fortunate that this film has its moments of unconscious humour, for otherwise it would be an intolerably morbid affair with its preoccupation with murder, the coffin and the grave'.

Bride of Frankenstein remains highly esteemed by modern film-watchers, and is generally ranked as one of the greatest horror movies, whenever such rankings are made. It is easy to see why; for one thing, it is one of the rare sequels that actually alters course from the original, expanding scale and style in surprising ways (as, say, *The Godfather, Part II* [1974] and *Mad Max II: The Road Warrior* [1982] would later). The postmodern nature of the picture probably accounts for its interest as well, the cheeky sense of self-commentary and the overtly campy humour being especially appealing in the early twenty-first century. The intense sympathy for the Monster is increased here, perhaps for the final time in a *Frankenstein* picture; the Monster learns to speak, to feel friendship and – pathetically – overhears the fact that he was created from dead flesh. The human nature of the Monster is frequently forgotten in the *Frankenstein* oeuvre, but when Karloff is shackled and bound by the villagers, his naked desperation reminds us that the Monster is a very confused human being.

Bride did not match *Frankenstein*'s box-office take and the horror genre went into a temporary wane (the boom-and-bust cycle in horror movie popularity has been consistent ever since). But the audience would not let the Monster go. It was not the Hollywood sequel-making machine that brought Karloff & Co. clomping back into the collective nightmare, but a relatively rare movie phenomenon at that time: the revival (aptly named, in this case).

THE MONSTER RALLIES

According to a merry *New York Times* writer in October 1938, as far as Universal had been concerned, the original *Dracula* and *Frankenstein* 'were reverently coiled up in their tin cans like a pair of anchovies and interred in dead storage to sleep the sleep of the just' (1938: 160). Then, sometime in the box-office doldrums of late summer, desperate exhibitors in Los Angeles and Seattle decided to disinter the two films and play them as a double bill. The key was the advertising: instead of playing down the terror, the promoters actively dared the audience to show up. 'Drac' and 'Frank', as they were quickly dubbed, swept the world as a double act.

The *Times* writer goes on: 'At the Viceroy Theatre in Salt Lake City the house was sold out by 10 o'clock in the morning. Four thousand frenzied Mormons milled around outside, finally broke through the police lines, smashed the plate glass box office, bent in the front doors and tore off one of the door checks in their eagerness to get in and be frightened.' In the course of a single revival season, the horror film had gone from a profitable aberration to a perennial. Is it a coincidence that the two films, originally hatched in the darkest moments of the Great Depression, re-emerged as the planet hurtled toward a World War that would dwarf the previous bloodbath? The *Times* wondered at 'this frantic public thirst for added su-

Newspaper advertisement for the 1938 re-release of *Frankenstein* and *Dracula*, daring the audience to attend; author's collection

pernatural horror in a world where natural horror is the make-up of every day's front page'.

Such questions were much in the mind of cultural commentators at the time. Writing in 1936, Andre Sennwald pondered the explicitness of recent horror, gangster and war films: 'It seems to me that this reversion to an almost morbid delight in witnessing the phenomena of pain, far from being an accidental and meaningless sort of thing, may be related very distinctly to the national state of mind.' (Sennwald's nation was the USA, but the idea applied even more urgently elsewhere.) 'The screen is providing an acute emotional experience and, what is more important, vast multitudes are enjoying it even in the act of being shocked and revolted by it' (1936: X5).

But remember, these hits were revivals: audiences were not flocking to see new terrors, but re-living the terrors they already knew. If the world was presenting a series of spiralling horrors that increased the average person's sense of helplessness, the thrills of the 1931 terror twins were within comprehensible boundaries. We had seen them; we had survived them; we could march through the ritual scares again knowing we would come into the daylight alive. (Not everybody was seeing the movies again, of course, and the pattern of re-release instigated by the 1938 double-bill would result in periodic indoctrinations of new generations of 11-year-olds into the fold.)

The stunning success of the *Dracula/Frankenstein* double bill inspired Universal to hatch *Son of Frankenstein* (1939), which lured Karloff back for one final lap in the heavy boots. James Whale was not involved, or even consulted. Colin Clive had died in 1937 at age 37, his death hastened considerably by acute alcohol abuse, so the new story drafted Basil Rathbone as the son of Henry Frankenstein. It was the beginning of a new wartime cycle of horror films for Universal, including the coining of a new character, *The Wolf Man* (1940), the resurrection of its Egyptian monster in a quartet of low-budget, low-comedy *Mummy* sequels, and a series of increasingly berserk vehicles for its marquee monsters, including the summit meetings of *Frankenstein Meets the Wolf Man* (1943) and *House of Frankenstein* (1944). The mythology of the Universal horror movies allowed for cross-breeding the monsters and the actors who played them; thus Count Dracula, the Wolf Man, and Frankenstein and his Monster could appear in the same picture.

Lon Chaney, Jr., having scored with lycanthropy in *The Wolf Man*, was cast as the Monster in *The Ghost of Frankenstein* (1942), but handed the role off to…Bela Lugosi, in *Frankenstein Meets the Wolf Man*, as Chaney obviously could not have played both roles in that one. (And so Lugosi deigned to wear the make-up at last.) Stuntman Glenn Strange was drafted to play the Monster in three subsequent Universal monster rallies of the 1940s – for a variety of reasons, including image rights, it is often Strange's face that adorns Universal's officially-sanctioned *Frankenstein* ancillary products today. Karloff did his best to keep from playing the Monster, although he was back in chummy company in *House of Frankenstein*, playing a mad doctor amidst the other monsters. (Karloff also participated in the best horror series of the 1940s, the low-budget run supervised by Val Lewton at RKO, which raised the bar on poetic treatments of horror; Karloff starred in three of the last titles in the run.) At Universal, *House of Dracula* (1945), a crazed hootenanny of the old gang, marked the last of the Frankenstein Monster's straight appearances, for a while.

I WAS A TEENAGE PHENOMENON

Given the many horror movie characters that flourished in this era, *Frankenstein* was obviously not alone in creating cult status; indeed, the entire 'golden era' of movie horror became something of a cult by the mid-1950s, and continues so today. But Frankenstein's Monster was the big one, somehow – the Clark Gable of movie monsters, the King of the unholy crew, the monster with the largest footprint, in every sense. Count Dracula had been out of the coffin first (even earlier than Lugosi's bow, if you count F.W. Murnau's unauthorised – and sublime – Bram Stoker rip-off from 1922, *Nosferatu*), but *Dracula* suffered from a scattered sequel history. Most likely because the literary property was still under copyright (unlike Mary Shelley's book), sequels to the 1931 hit were a stop-and-start process; *Dracula's Daughter* (1936), officially based on a separate Stoker story, lacked Lugosi, while MGM's *Return of the Vampire* (1935), with Lugosi striding through cobwebs amidst Tod Browning's direction, was a clear attempt to catch some of the *Dracula* mojo. Universal's *Son of Dracula* would not spring to life until 1943, with the ever-flexible Lon Chaney, Jr., trying out the cape.

Perhaps more than the staggered production history of *Dracula* sequels, and despite the enduring popularity of vampire movies in general, there was something a little bit effete about Dracula himself, despite the avowed thirst for blood. *Frankenstein*, however, was unequivocal in its fear factor, despite the shadings of Karloff's performance and the sympathy of James Whale's treatment. If a cult is worth its salt, it is durable, and the *Frankenstein* cult never really waned, regardless of cinematic or social trends. Thus, when Universal's run of straight horror had ground down, the Monster was the first target of lampoonery for the studio's contract comedians, Bud Abbott and Lou Costello. *Abbott and Costello Meet Frankenstein* (1948) was a surprise box-office hit that ushered in a series of standoffs against the Invisible Man, Dr. Jekyll and Mr. Hyde, the Mummy, and the laboriously titled *Abbott and Costello Meet the Killer, Boris Karloff* (1949), the latter demonstrating the reach of Karloff's association with mayhem. (The fact of Karloff being a brand-name-worthy commodity had earlier been proven in the enormously popular play *Arsenic and Old Lace* [1941; filmed 1944] in which one of the sinister characters is referred to as resembling an actor like Boris Karloff – a joke doubled, at least in the original stage production, by the fact that Karloff was playing the role.)

Abbott and Costello Meet Frankenstein actually gathers the Monster, Count Dracula (Lugosi back in the role), and the Wolf Man, although it is a measure of the Universal monsters' pecking order that the only name in the title belongs to the big F. The comedic intent of the thing indicated Universal's exhaustion with the classic form, although horror itself would remain a mainstay of their low-budget operations. By the 1950s, Universal seemed to have abandoned its essential stable of monsters, churning out bargain-basement horror titles such as *Monster on the Campus* (1958) and *The Thing*

That Couldn't Die. At that point, teen subculture and horror movies were meshing, requiring a steady stream of fare for drive-ins and disreputable grindhouses.

In 1957, the 'Drac' and 'Frank' revival phenomenon of twenty years earlier was repeated in a new way. Universal released a package of 52 of its horror pictures for syndication to US television; they called it the 'Shock!' collection, although different local stations broadcast the films under various names. A flood of vintage horror hit the airwaves, and its smash success startled TV programmers and cultural observers alike. Ratings shot up everywhere the movies were broadcast – at one point Sacramento's horror movie slot was capturing 79 percent of viewers in its market – and a new phenomenon, the horror-movie host, was born. Local actors or part-time station managers would dress in ghoulish costumes, introduce the films, and occasionally insinuate themselves into the movies, spoofing the decidedly non-classic nature of many of the titles. The hosts would have to work particularly hard to generate some excitement around sleepy, non-horror items such as *Secret of the Chateau* (1934) and *Chinatown Squad* (1935), a phenomenon later captured by the comedy series *SCTV*, which had its horror-movie host, Count Floyd, habitually apologising for movies that were not actually scary. Some hosts became hugely popular local celebrities; when San Francisco's 'Terrence' idly called for students to rally on the University of California campus, 1200 hundred people showed up, and police were needed to send away the mob.

A *Saturday Evening Post* article about the craze reported that 'In some cities, the weirdie films earned ratings for their stations 10 to 12 times what they had been', and observed that the fans of such shows came from across the age spectrum: adults who had grown up with the films, college kids, and children seeing them for the first time. The *Post* even persuaded the esteemed social scientist Margaret Mead to weigh in, and she was sanguine, even approving, on the subject: 'The monsters and mummies on the screen, which are always destroyed in the end just as the heroine is saved, are a relief from everyday horror' (Tunley 1958: 18–21).

'Shock!' inspired other monster-related phenomena, notably the debut of Forrest J. Ackerman's influential magazine *Famous Monsters of Filmland*, which launched in February 1958. Because the consumers of 'Shock!' and *Famous Monsters* and their ilk included the likes of Steven Spielberg, George Lucas, and dozens of other future filmmakers, this revival of horror was in some ways the most decisive moment in the continuation of the cult. Television, comic books, and fan magazines brought the cult to countless more households, yet the new accessibility actually perpetuated the outlaw nature of it. Late-night or Saturday-afternoon monster movies were the province of the young, and official disapproval, from schoolteachers or clergy, meant a kid was on the right track.

And so the talismanic power of the Monster's image, and the name 'Frankenstein', was renewed. The word itself is potent – Frankenstein – with its strong Teutonic cadence draped around a hard 'k' sound in the middle; in the miasmic world of European low-budget horror, for instance, it might be dropped into the umpteenth alternate title of a film having nothing to do with mad scientists or reanimated cadavers, let alone a connection to Mary Shelley.

It is a pre-sold brand name, as a sudden eruption of F-titles in the youth market of 1957–58 proved. *I Was a Teenage Frankenstein* was released in the fall of 1957, shortly after the surprise success of producer Herman Cohen's *I Was a Teenage Werewolf*. That the title *I Was a Teenage Frankenstein* blithely continues the decades-old confusion between the names of the Monster and its creator should not cloud its marketing genius; the words are built for a mid-1950s drive-in theatre marquee. Similarly, *Frankenstein's*

Daughter (1958) blends early rock movie devices (lover's lane, nightclub combo) with an old-school monster story. The skeleton of each film is remarkably consistent with *Frankenstein* canonical thought: *IWATF* has Dr. Frankenstein (Whit Bissell) a descendant of the famous scientific family, and the tropes of the European Gothic (there is even an alligator pit below the laboratory) are transplanted to Eisenhower-era America. *Frankenstein's Daughter* has another member of the family (Donald Murphy), here disguised as Dr. Frank, meddling in his ancestors' business and causing harm in the US suburbs. For *Frankenstein 1970* (1958), the story remained in Europe and had the added benefit of Boris Karloff in the role of Baron Frankenstein, this time hosting the crew of a low-budget filmmaking unit in his family abode – a good opportunity for the Baron to take up re-animation himself.

All these B-movie flowerings of the F-myth were part of a major rejuvenation of the cult – and demonstrate how each historical moment gets the *Frankenstein* it needs. Britain's Hammer Films re-defined its identity by turning to Shelley's novel and (under the careful gaze of Universal Pictures' lawyers) doing the origin story again. The film that resulted, *The Curse of Frankenstein* (1957), became an enormous hit, establishing a formula and filmmaking team (director Terence Fisher, writer Jimmy Sangster, stars Peter Cushing and Christopher Lee) that would fuel the studio's busy output of horror pictures over the next decade and a half – including six *Frankenstein* sequels.

Curse displays the basics of what would be Hammer's approach for the series: the *décor* and manners of an English drawing room drama, incongruously leading to revelations of severed heads and unspeakable experiments. (Hammer's *Frankenstein* series made its fortune in the repeated spectacle of eyeballs and brains plopping into glass containers.) *Curse* catches many of the era's at-large concerns, such as atomic-age anxiety about science overstepping its bounds and post-Holocaust revulsion at ideas of eugenics (the Baron is a fan of genetic engineering). But it's also got some of the self-criticism loose in British culture at the time, and nearly plays as a parody of a certain kind of respectable Brit picture; one scene opens with Baron Frankenstein (Cushing in his career-making role) at breakfast with his fiancée Elizabeth, wordlessly preparing his toast and politely asking Elizabeth to pass the marmalade – a scene made blackly funny by the one that precedes it, in which the Baron has lured his maid/mistress to violent death at the hands of his creation (Lee).

Twenty-five years after the 1931 original, the cult of *Frankenstein* had become incredibly defined, so that each manifestation can be counted on to march through similar conventions. The relationship of the word 'cult' to its religious meaning is useful here. Anyone buying a ticket for a *Frankenstein* movie in 1957 could assume certain liturgical notes being sounded in the course of the ceremony, whether the film was *The Curse of Frankenstein* or *I Was a Teenage Frankenstein*: an isolated laboratory; an obsessed doctor/scientist (the questing Prometheus of Shelley/Whale's story was now mostly replaced by a wicked egomaniac with god-like ambitions); the search for body parts, often including a damaged brain; grisly medical detail; an annoyingly unhelpful colleague (*Curse*'s Robert Urquhart is especially irritating in this regard) to provide the 'voice of reason' and delay the audience's enjoyment of the experiment; lab effects; and a Monster, preferably of ingenious and horrifying design.

Those not initiated in the cult might deride these conventions. Believers understand that the conventions are very much the point. The similarities from film to film create a feeling of inclusiveness in the process – indeed, fans tend to be disturbed by violent shifts away from the core ceremonies.

WHAT HUMP?

The Monster could emerge in movies that had nothing ostensibly to do with *Frankenstein* stories. Karloff himself put on the make-up again for a TV episode of *Route 66*, to cite one example. At times movies offered up evidence that the Monster had secured his place in our collective unconscious, nowhere more hauntingly than in *The Night of the Hunter* (1955), the only film directed by Charles Laughton. At times, Robert Mitchum's homicidal preacher is shot and lit as though to conjure up memories of *Frankenstein*; as critic Richard T. Jameson beautifully insists, 'When he plunges, stiff-armed and black-coated, into the river after the children's skiff, his appearance and his depraved, unreasoning animal cries ring familiar: he does not even resemble – he *is* Karloff's Frankenstein monster' (undated: 2). Laughton had worked with Whale on *The Old Dark House* and, bisexual himself, was married for decades to Elsa Lanchester, Frankenstein's bride.

That film was a masterpiece; but the Monster would travel through less glorious mutations in the 1960s and 1970s, from astounding variations such as *Jesse James Meets Frankenstein's Daughter* (1966) to softcore porn Euro-trash translations of the myth. Yet the integrity of the Karloff-Whale original, the Jack Pierce make-up with the flattop head, remained intact. The Monster became an increasingly visible image as the 'monster kids' of the late 1950s and 1960s embraced the icon. Like religious trinkets sold at holy sites, Frankenstein's monster could be seen in playing cards, soaps, candy dispensers, plastic Halloween candy buckets. The crowning achievement of this movement was Aurora Models' wildly successful line of monster model kits, the author's obsession with which is described in Chapter One. These plastic figures began in 1961 (Frankenstein's Monster was the first offering) and remained popular well into the

1970s, occasionally being revived thereafter. That a kid buying a monster kit in 1971 was embracing a 40-year-old icon did not seem to matter, since the movie itself was still available on TV and the monster image ubiquitous.

Universal steered back to the Abbott and Costello route with the launch in 1964 of an unlikely television sitcom, *The Munsters*, which used the Jack Pierce make-up for the bumbling-dad character of Herman Munster (Fred Gwynne), a typical TV father who happens to look like the Frankenstein Monster. The appropriation of the Monster as a safe figure of family fun would continue through the manufacture of cartoons and action figures through the 1970s and 80s. Kids of the early Seventies would be introduced to the high-sugar cereals Franken Berry and Count Chocula, which made the images of the famous monsters safe for consumption (in every sense of the word) by children. Franken Berry used a pink cartoon variation of the Monster to promote its strawberry-flavoured cereal.

The Monster could crop up anywhere in the reference-happy postmodern era – thus the rock star from California married by The Who's 'Sally Simpson' (via Ken Russell's wild visualisation in the movie *Tommy*, 1975) appeared as the Frankenstein Monster, clad in gold lamé suit and cowboy hat. The Monster found himself folded into the Japanese monster-movie universe, in *Frankenstein Conquers the World* (1966). Under Andy Warhol's aegis, director Paul Morrissey would create *Flesh for Frankenstein* (1973), a madcap high-camp treatment of the story with explicit gore and 3D effects. The estimable *littérateur* Christopher Isherwood (writing with longtime partner Don Bachardy) wrote a three-hour TV movie called *Frankenstein: The True Story* (1973), which despite its presumptuous title departed considerably from Shelley's novel, especially in the depiction of the Monster as an initially beautiful man who gradually decomposes into hideousness.

The latter two adaptations had strong gay overtones. And 'overtones' is hardly a sufficient word for what happened to the Frankenstein myth in *The Rocky Horror Picture Show* (1975), itself based on a stage musical called *The Rocky Horror Show*. This uproarious revue, the brainchild of writer-composer-actor Richard O'Brien, is a parody of horror movies, especially B-pictures seen late at night on TV; its central mad doctor is called Frank N. Furter, a transvestite labouring over his creature for his own reasons: 'I've been making a man/With blond hair and a tan/And he's good for relieving my tension.' A flop on its initial release, *Rocky Horror* came to define the cult movie phenomenon: building a fan base by word of mouth, creating a sensation at endless midnight screenings, inspiring its devotees to dress in costume and ritualistically participate during showings. Such is the reach of *Frankenstein*: it is a lab out of which other cult phenomena might rise.

The most visible result of the revising phase of the *Frankenstein* mythos was Mel Brooks's spoof, *Young Frankenstein*, a funny and affectionate variation on the story. So complete was Brooks's (and co-writer/star Gene Wilder's) homage to the original Universal films that Kenneth Strickfaden's instruments from the 1931 film were leased for use in the movie's laboratory sequences. Implicit in the film's success was the knowledge that the audience would understand all the references; they had grown up with the *Frankenstein* pictures and would be able to savour the jokes.

The parody was all the more lethal for being so exact – just as Brooks's *Blazing Saddles* (1973) nearly finished off the western genre. In the final chapter we will see how the *Frankenstein* phenomenon has weathered the last couple of decades, but first it is time to journey into the 1931 film itself, to poke into the mysteries of what happened at Goldstadt Medical College and an abandoned windmill and how a monster became a headliner on the world cultural stage.

4

BEYOND THE CLOUDS AND STARS:
SURVEYING *FRANKENSTEIN*

In some ways it is the most startling moment of *Frankenstein*, a film that contains a series of shocks for viewers. The climax of the picture has arrived, and Henry Frankenstein's monster has dragged his creator to a windmill, chased there by cinema's greatest Mob of Angry Villagers. Inside the mill, the Monster pulls the unconscious scientist to the top level, where a great wheel is grinding on its side, turned by the windmill's tattered struts. Henry Frankenstein awakens, and he tussles with the Monster; in one suspended moment they face each other, through the gears of the turning wheel. Vertical beams sweep past first Henry's face, and then the Monster's, their images matched in an almost seamless cut, and for a heartbeat, their faces seem to blend into the same person.

This is a shivery, richly suggestive moment, and its theme is consistent with a longstanding *doppelgänger* tradition in *Frankenstein* properties, from Mary Shelley onward (quite explicit, for instance, in the 1910 Edison film of the story): that Frankenstein and his creation are two sides of the same

Zoetrope effect: matched cuts of maker (Colin Clive) and monster (Boris Karloff), seen through the gears of the mill

personality, acting out light and dark, conscious and subconscious, impulses. But there's more: the moving vertical slats of the millworks, slapping across the frame like optical 'wipes,' are the visual equivalent of a Zoetrope or Stroboscope – or a flip book – the primitive early forms of motion pictures. Thus when Frankenstein's face is replaced by the Monster's, for a second we do not notice the change, and a tragic relationship is fused just before everything goes up in flames. (It might be the greatest example of self-referential image-making in *le cinema fantastique* until the 'lens' of the alien's heart closes its aperture in *E.T.* [1982].)

Along with summing up one of the film's strongest themes, this sequence should also lay to rest any doubts about director James Whale's status as a conscious artist. Whale's films have a curious sense of both the archaic and the modern about them, but the evidence (both on the screen and from contemporaries who worked with him) suggests that Whale was savvy about the language of cinema and controlling in his methods to achieve effects. As well as being a director's film, *Frankenstein* is also a movie of its era, of its (hardly top-rung) studio, and of its genre – a genre it helped invent and codify. And like many films, the final results are significantly different from the initial edit of the movie; studio nervousness, official censorship, and test-audience response all played a role in forming the final 71-minute *Frankenstein*...and even *that* version was subject to various cuts and dialogue elisions through the years.

The very first thing that comes onscreen in *Frankenstein* is itself a product of post-production tinkering. As described in Chapter Two, a prologue was shot some weeks after the initial production of the film had ended. Roman Catholic authorities in Canada had voiced objections to the film's depiction of Henry Frankenstein's challenge to God, concerns echoed by Los Angeles Catholics; Universal execs felt that a spoken introduction, condemning Frankenstein's irreligious hubris, would mitigate the horrors to come, or at least give the studio an 'out' when it came to criticism of the film's content.

One could compare this device to the scenes added to the Howard Hughes/Howard Hawks *Scarface* (1930–32) for fear the audience would become inappropriately excited by the gangster hero. Without Hawks's participation, a new written introduction and clumsy new scenes were added, informing the audience they really should not be identifying with or rooting for the charismatic criminal at the centre of the story.

The *Frankenstein* introduction is a far cry from those sober-sided scenes. Edward Van Sloan, who plays Dr. Waldman in the film, breezes out from behind a curtain to address the audience. His puckish attitude suggests that he knows, and he knows that we know, that what he is saying is designed not to warn but to titillate us. After telling us that we may be thrilled, shocked, and horrified by what we are about to see, he adds, 'So if any of you feel that you do not care to subject your nerves to such a strain, now is your chance to....Well... we've warned you....' No one ever gets up from their theatre seat; no one ever turns off the TV. The distinguished Mr. Van Sloan ends his little speech with a twinkle and a shrug. This is not a warning; this is an invitation.

More than that, too. This outside-the-movie introduction increases the sense of ceremony that attends *Frankenstein*. Van Sloan looks like the theatre manager coming out to politely inform the audience of some urgent information, but he is also the priest closing the circle before the rite begins. The film cannot simply start; it needs an incantation first. And in the horror movie universe, Van Sloan's presence is another element that makes us feel we are in the cult: he is the indelible Dr. Abraham Van Helsing from *Dracula*, the small, careful academic who faces down the vampire. He would repeat the role in *Dracula's Daughter* and play a similar monster-fighter in *The Mummy*. Outside of Universal horror, Van Sloan had a minor screen career, but because of his proximity to the monsters, he is, as the sideshow performers chant in *Freaks*, 'One of us, one of us'.

The opening credits of *Frankenstein* blend German Expressionist design with an Art Deco look not uncommon in the early 1930s. Behind the title cards is a bizarre drawing of a figure with clawlike hands and eyes that shoot out beams of light. It is not an image contained in the movie, but the prominence of eyes and hands signals the importance of two of James Whale's most insistent motifs. The following title cards, in which 'Mrs. Percy B. Shelley' is credited with the source novel, are foregrounded against dozens of eyes swirling around the face of a menacing-looking bald man.

The film has barely begun, and already the credits refer to the unfortunate new being as a Monster. This is key: the absence of a name already makes him a bastard; we are never told the names of the people whose body parts have been joined and animated to form this giant, so he lacks any kind of genea-logical index, except for the stitching and jolting provided by Frankenstein. (Indeed Henry Frankenstein pointedly corrects Dr. Waldman's assertion that he is trying to bring a dead body back to life: 'That body's not dead. It has never lived. I created it and made it with my own hands.') The Monster's anonymity carries through most of the movie adaptations of the story, al-though in the pilot episode of a proposed Hammer Pictures TV series called 'Tales of Frankenstein' the Monster is referred to as 'Helmut'. Long before the 1931 film was made, the Monster was being erroneously referred to as 'Frankenstein', and the glut of lazily-titled B-movies has hopelessly muddled the issue.

If Frankenstein and the Monster are linked as a personality, a Jekyll and Hyde before Robert Louis Stevenson concocted his double man, then this naming confusion makes sense. Maybe that is another reason Frankenstein (Shelley's Victor F. or Whale's Henry F.) never names his creation; he senses the being is not separate at all. In the Shelley novel, Victor goes out for one of his frequent treks (a great deal of the book is long-distance walking of the Romantic variety) the morn-ing after bringing his creation to life. He has a strong feeling of the uncanny, and flashes on a passage from Coleridge's 'Rime of the Ancient Mariner':

Like one who, on a lonely road,
 Doth walk in fear and dread,
And, having once turned round, walks on,
 And turns no more his head;
Because he knows a frightful fiend
 Doth close behind him tread.

That uncanny follower is one's own shadow, and the book is easily read as Victor's feverish anxiety about his dual nature. Curiously, when the Monster takes over the novel's narrative voice, he echoes the Coleridge quote, but with a different slant: 'When I looked around I saw and heard none like me. Was I, then, a monster, a blot upon the earth, from which all men fled and whom all men disowned?' The Monster does not carry the unnamed fear that Frankenstein has; he is wretched, but he does not have the luxury of an average person's free-floating angst. His resentments are quite specific. When he and Frankenstein meet, the scientist rages ('Begone, vile insect!') and threatens to kill his creation, while the Monster's first words to him are 'I expected this reception,' followed by an eloquent, if forceful, demand to be heard.

In Whale's vision, Henry Frankenstein begins the film as a fallen figure, already skulking about a clammy graveyard in search of a corpse – an introduction almost as superb as the later arrival of the Monster. The first image in the film proper is a close-up of a pair of hands pulling a rope from a grave, as bells ring and someone intones Latin. Although a different establishing shot of the mourners was originally planned to open the film (it was later employed in *Bride of Frankenstein*), this moment introduces *Frankenstein*'s unusual emphasis on hands, as well as the recurring use of bell sounds at crucial moments. The shot moves up and then laterally across the faces of mourners at this gravesite, including an oddly diffident clergyman, a tilted cross, and a funerary statue of Death. A somewhat abrupt cut puts us at the edge of an iron railing, behind which the bulging-eyed face of Fritz (Dwight Frye), a hunchback, is rising into close-up. A beat later, the head of Henry Frankenstein (Colin Clive) appears behind Fritz, and Frankenstein's hands press down on Fritz's shoulders. Or his hump, more precisely. 'Down, down you fool,' whispers Henry, as Fritz descends out of frame, and Henry's face hangs for a moment in the gloom of the shot, looking as gaunt and spectral as the nearby Death statue.

These opening shots are very visibly choreographed; there is nothing stock about them. As that first tracking shot moves across its line of tilted verticals and slanted hillside, the sense of an off-kilter world is strong; we are slipping off the edges of the frame. The crucifix and the Death statue flicker past, equally weighted, as though vying for our attention, and they initiate themes of resurrection and the triumph over death – but hardly in the respectful way suggested by Edward Van Sloan's opening warning. The whole set is clearly on a soundstage, which only enhances the claustrophobic mood, the sickly grey light that feeds this crepuscular scene. The sky is a painted scrim, its fold and wrinkles visible, appropriate enough for a movie in which the theatrical nature of the presentation (commented upon by Frankenstein himself at times) is part of the ritual. And when we meet Henry Frankenstein and Fritz, their deliberate up-and-down movement puns on the film's repeating image of Henry raising and lowering things – a self-appointed god who brings his creation up and then lowers him again. Why be a god unless you can cast your favourites out of heaven?

After the close-up of Fritz and Henry there is a cut to another lateral shot, this one reversing direction from the opener, finding the mourners trailing away from the gravesite, leaving a homely gravedigger to begin spading dirt into the hole. The loud thwack of the earth hitting the casket is especially jarring (1931 was still very much the early-sound era, and someone on the *Frankenstein* set had the bright idea to put a microphone inside the coffin); the equally earthy gesture of the gravedigger flicking his match into the grave after lighting his pipe is a typically macabre Whale touch. Like the title character, this fellow does not respect Death much either.

For his part, Fritz nimbly hops on top of the grave mound to begin digging, and Henry manages to send his first shovelful of dirt into the face of the statue of Death. *Frankenstein* is a systemically irreverent movie, an attitude that would become more pronounced in the whimsicalities of *Bride of Frankenstein*. As the two men heft the coffin free from the soil, Fritz lets loose with a cheerful, 'Here he comes!' The coffin sits on its end, Henry cradling it, patting his enormous hands on its wood with something like parental affection. 'He's just resting,' Henry says, 'waiting for a new life to come.' Like much that follows, the moment seems to hover somewhere between humour and madness, but a man who has waited all day to exhume a fresh corpse can be forgiven for a temporary derangement from reality. And note the tender use of 'he' as a pronoun for this cadaver – and yet Henry will later shout, 'It's alive!' when his assembled 'son' quivers his hands for the first time.

One can imagine the effect this sequence had on audiences that first saw it: grave robbers scuttling around a cemetery, and one of them is the *hero*? Still, the next scene tops it. The night dark now, the carcass-hunting duo pull their wagon up to a gallows, where a hanged man still dangles. The well-born Henry is smartly turned out in tweed jacket and an ascot tied around his own neck. We have a chance to appreciate this in the second before the body drops from the gibbet, past Henry, to land with a thump at his feet (another of the film's many descents). The scene ends on a medium close-up of Henry, having examined the body. 'The neck's broken,' he says, disgusted. 'The brain is useless. We must find another brain.'

The last line is delivered as Frankenstein looks off in the middle-distance, which happens to be almost into the camera, and it hangs in the air as the screen fades to black. It is spoken with intensity and utter sincerity: throughout *Frankenstein* (and even in the campy setting of *Bride of Frankenstein*), Colin Clive's performance remains free of irony. Yet this deadpan declaration has mischief behind it, as though Whale were tweaking our already traumatised sensibilities. 'We must find another brain'? What kind of movie have we walked in on?

But this is not yet the moment for exposition. The film fades up on a sign that reads, 'Goldstadt Medical College', which dissolves into a wide shot of a lecture room. Dr. Waldman and his assistants have finished a demonstration with a cadaver, and while the preceding two scenes might have prepared us for this subject matter, Whale is not finished with a certain deadpan humor. The elegantly composed wide shot of the room is replaced by a blunt set-up at the level of the cadaver's bare feet, which stick out at us as the assistants cover the body with a sheet. At that point, one of the medicos walks past a lab skeleton hanging near the body, and jostles it so that it bounces – an echo of the previous scene, when Fritz, to his utter terror, brushed by the hanged man and made him swing. (Fritz is right to fear hanging, of course – his own destiny awaits him shortly.)

What follows is a heavily debated sequence in *Frankenstein*iana. Waldman displays a pair of jars; one contains a normal brain, the other an abnormal brain. He explains that the bad brain exhibits characteristics that are consistent with a life made up 'of brutality, of violence and murder'. Fritz, who sneaks into the lecture room after class is over, will seize the jar with the good brain but – at the inopportune sound of a gong – drop and shatter it. The abnormal brain is still intact, so he grabs it and scampers out. (How many movie mad scientists have been undercut by incompetent assistants?) Henry Frankenstein will not learn of the mistake – we assume Fritz has the presence of mind, and the survival instincts, to remove the label on the jar that reads ABNORMAL BRAIN – until Waldman informs him of which brain went missing.

The abnormal brain has no correlative in the Shelley novel, nor, apparently, in the stage versions of the book. It entered the screenplay around the time James Whale took over the project. Some *Frankenstein* commentators suggest that the abnormal brain negates the entire science experiment at the heart of the story – Frankenstein was doomed from the beginning, and the Monster's late rampaging can be chalked up to a criminal mind. David Skal suggests that the gimmick subverts the meaning of Shelley's original, because now 'it is not Henry's divine presumption that sets in motion the catastrophe, but a deception and cover-up by a handicapped employee'. The success or failure of the experiment cannot be accurately measured, because the variables were screwed from the start.

In their book *Popular Eugenics*, Susan Currell and Christina Cogdell find *Frankenstein* to be a ripe text for the ideas and anxieties about eugenics that were floating around the culture at the time; Waldman's speech about brain shape is an example of a eugenicist rhapsodising about his subject. It is a fruitful angle on the movie, and certainly the Monster represents a collection of disturbing, and thus frightening, 'subnormal' characteristics – disfigured facial and cranial features, spastic body movements, and signs of mental retardation (although that has to do with the Monster's instantly grown-up body housing a brain that is, apparently, learning like a child). The fact that *Frankenstein* was released as Adolf Hitler was climbing the rungs of political power in Germany has long been a source of interest for scholars, and the film's spectacle of an intense genius labouring away (in Germany) in immoral medical experiments might seem to rhyme with some of the pseudo-scientific insanity that would lead the Nazis to develop their ideas of racial purity and social engineering.

But wait. In the body of *Frankenstein* itself, the subject of the abnormal brain is only briefly referred to after the lecture-hall sequence. In a crucial and lyrically written scene, Henry Frankenstein and Waldman talk about the newly-made Monster, with the older doctor urging Frankenstein to destroy it. This is when Henry learns the stolen brain came from a criminal, as Waldman emphasises the deterministic hopelessness of dealing with such a sensibility. Henry's response, considering the weight given to the labelling bungle during the theft scene, is surprisingly sanguine: nonplussed for a moment, he glances over his shoulder towards the part of the castle where the Monster is presumably looming (Colin Clive plays the reaction to a fare-thee-well) and then responds, 'Oh well – after all, it's only a piece of dead tissue.' A few moments later, he takes the nurture-over-nature position: 'He's only a few days old, remember. So far he's been kept in complete darkness. Wait 'til I bring him into the light.' Whatever his ostensible crimes against God's law and the natural way, Frankenstein shows himself to be a far more modern and forward-looking scientist than Waldman, that official voice of order and sanity.

As Henry Frankenstein shrugs off the supposed calamity of the abnormal brain, so does the movie. Neither in the writing of the role nor in Boris Karloff's performance is there evidence of a reflexively criminal personality in the Monster; the film goes to some lengths to show that his violent actions are the result of defending himself against the cruel taunting of Fritz, as well as the larger issue of his hurt at being rejected by his creator. The Monster throws a little girl into a lake, but out of pure innocence, and his reaction is visible terror. His later stalking of Elizabeth is perhaps an attempt to eliminate a rival in Frankenstein's affections, as children will fantasise doing with stepparents. But in the sequence in which Henry finally does let the Monster 'into the light', the newborn creature's infant-like reactions – grasping at the sunshine that pours from a lofty skylight, moaning with curiosity and pleasure – are hardly the criminal-brain stuff of Waldman's social Darwinism, and instantly elicit our pity.

So is the abnormal brain idea a mistake, a late-in-the-day screenwriter's notion that muddies the film's theme? Later *Frankenstein* sequels take up the thread; near the beginning of *Son of Frankenstein*, family scion Wolf Frankenstein (Basil Rathbone) declares that the bad brain was entirely responsible for the disaster of his father's otherwise brilliant experiment. And of course Mel Brooks would create a choice moment from the abnormal brain confusion in *Young Frankenstein*, as hunchbacked assistant Eye-gore insists that the brain comes from someone named 'Abby Normal'. The textual evidence of *Frankenstein* itself suggests that Waldman's brief on eugenics is simply wrong, and that the brain inside the Monster's head is, at the least, childlike, and perhaps completely amnesiac (thus the Monster is like the hero of a dozen post-World War II film noirs, wandering around trying to puzzle out what exactly got him into this strange mess). Certainly the scene with the brains is dramatically shrewd, if childhood experience counts for anything – I will never forget the original shudder of realising that Fritz has unknowingly done something calamitous in his haste.

Talking of the Monster's air of deformity brings up a persistent theme in the Frankenstein mythos as a whole: the frequency of misshapenness and disfigurement in the sequels and remakes. Aside from the Monster, the series is populated with all kinds of 'nature's mistakes' (as the alternate title to *Freaks* described the deformed and disabled): the blind hermit in *Bride of Frankenstein*, the broken-necked Ygor and the one-armed Krogh in *Son of Frankenstein*, the disfigured barmaid in *Frankenstein Created Woman*, even a Vietnam amputee in the abysmal *Blackenstein* (1973). And, of course, beginning with Fritz there is a parade of hunchbacks, frequently abused with the promise that the scientific experiments will be used to repair their bowed spines: it happens in *House of Frankenstein*, *House of Dracula*, and Hammer's *The Revenge of Frankenstein* (1958).

This obsession with society's shunned people brings us back to one of the basic tensions between the Monster and the viewer, and Monster and maker. Ostensibly he frightens us because he might harm us, yet he is not quick of foot or particularly keen of strategy. No, there is something deeper in the fear we feel about the Monster, and it is connected to his condition, his distorted appearance that makes us pity him, sympathise with him, yet not akin to him. It is by now a commonplace observation that we fear the Other because in our nearness to him, we risk becoming infected by him; his deformity might transfer to us. Even seeing such a monster on a movie screen provokes, at the level of 'there but for the grace of God go I', the shiver of the uncanny that attends seeing such a person. As Freud wrote in *The Uncanny*, of the inexplicable eeriness of witnessing, say, someone afflicted by madness: 'Here the layman sees a manifestation of forces that he did not suspect in a fellow human being, but whose stirrings he can dimly perceive in remote corners of his own personality.' Mary Shelley's Victor Frankenstein instantly rejects his creation – a bizarre reaction, even given the new man's repulsive appearance. Would not Frankenstein have had some residual amount of the cold curiosity of the scientist? Or was part of his flight a result of looking at his worst fear about himself?

THE FAMILY FRANKENSTEIN

Heredity counts less than parenting in *Frankenstein*'s world – even if the many sequels and remakes suggest that the name 'Frankenstein' comes with a galloping family lunacy attached. There is the slightest hint of Henry's relationship with his own father in the aforementioned conversation with Waldman. 'My father,' Henry says with a bitter chuckle, 'never believes in anyone.' Now, the Baron Frankenstein (Frederick Kerr) functions mostly as the film's comic relief, a doddering fuddy-duddy, so no serious reading need be called out here; still, the flicker of irritation on Henry's face is authentic, and when the Baron is confronted by Elizabeth and Victor Moritz about Henry's mysterious laboratory project, the Baron huffs, 'You think I'm an idiot, don't you? But I'm not,' and proceeds to dismiss his son's experiments as so much nonsense, especially when there is the wedding with Elizabeth to plan.

Henry's own failure as a parent is part of a larger scheme in the film, of control. Beginning with Henry's first domineering push of Fritz, the movie sets up a series of power relationships. Henry's creation of a new man is perhaps the ultimate example of one person attempting to exert control over another (and over life itself). Fritz, for his part, has displayed no signs of cruelty – in fact, he has been a sometimes amusing figure – until the Monster's arrival. Suddenly, Fritz is taunting the Monster, waving a torch in his face. In the land of the monsters the hunchbacked man is king.

Henry does not merely create the Monster to exercise control. He might be proving his father, who never believes in anyone, wrong. What other pressures are there on Henry Frankenstein? He is wealthy, and apparently has no constraints on living space or the purchase of some rather elaborate laboratory equipment. Everyone thinks he is brilliant. And he is about to get married. Hmmm … instead of concentrating on plans for the wedding, Henry deliberately runs off and tries to invent a man out of dead parts, a man who ends up embodying a certain wildness – a reversion to childhood feelings and wants, as opposed to adult responsibilities.

As Robin Wood – a critic whose writing on the horror film is always suggestive – has written about the doubling of Frankenstein and the Monster: 'But we should be alerted to the relationship's true significance from the moment in the James Whale original where Frankenstein's decision to create his monster is juxtaposed very precisely with his decision to become engaged. The doppelganger motif reveals the Monster as normality's shadow' (1979: 7–28). And Henry Frankenstein does not seek normality.

In that same crucial scene with Waldman, Henry waxes lyrical about the source of his ambitions. 'Poor old Waldman,' he smiles, listening to the staid warnings from his former teacher. 'Have you never wanted to do anything that was dangerous? Where should we be if nobody tried to find out what lies beyond? Have you never wanted to look beyond the clouds and the stars? Or to know what causes the trees to bud, or what changes a darkness into light? But if you talk like that, people call you crazy. Well if I could discover just one of these things – what Eternity is for example – I wouldn't care if they did call me crazy.' These lines were not in any of the screenplay drafts prior to shooting, a hint that they had a special point for James Whale, beyond the standard this-might-be-madness-but-where's-your-scientific-curiosity scene, which would work its way into many future mad-scientist pictures.

Whale has already limned the difference between Frankenstein and Waldman in a typically skillful way. Henry is a figure of verticality; in the opening graveyard scene, Colin Clive's rail-thin figure rhymes easily with the crosses and monuments that stab the landscape like sticks in a pincushion. He is consistently associated with the high verticals of the laboratory, both the outside tower and the inside's vertiginous, gurney-boosting center.

Waldman, on the other hand, is a horizontal man, introduced in his office in a scene so rigorously composed by Whale and cinematographer Arthur Edeson it practically throttles the old geezer. Frankenstein's fiancée, Elizabeth (Mae Clarke), and his best friend Victor Moritz (John Boles), are sitting in Waldman's office, discussing what to do about Henry. The sequence opens with a shot that includes all three people grouped around Waldman's desk. The frame is dominated by

Elizabeth (Mae Clarke) and Victor (John Boles) visit the fussy, horizontal realm of Dr. Waldman (Edward Van Sloan)

different strata of horizontal lines: the desk itself, a row of test tubes atop the desk, the shelves behind Waldman and the books lined on a couple of them – and, gloriously, a row of human skulls lined up on yet another shelf. Waldman is like a relic silted over by generations of academic thought, trapped under layers of sediment; his companion is a skull perched on his desk, a *memento mori* that Whale mockingly places opposite Waldman's head in a later shot in this scene. Edward Van Sloan's delivery of certain juicy lines ('Herr Frankenstein is greatly changed') is beyond plummy – 'pruney' is more like it – and he almost reiterates his out-of-character speech from the prologue, as he agrees, against his better judgment, to accompany Elizabeth and Victor out to Henry's lab: 'Very well, Fräulein, I've warned you. But if you wish it, I will go.'

This scene, and the scene before it, are sandwiched in as 'breathing room' in *Frankenstein*'s rapid series of opening unpleasantries. When we last saw Fritz, skulking out of the Medical School lecture room with the Abnormal Brain jar under his hump – er, arm – the grave-robbing sequences were coming to a close. (And by the way, the absence of music here, the echo-ey sound of Fritz clumping up the classroom stairs, is a key to the effectiveness of the scene. The hush of *Frankenstein*, and *Dracula*, has a great deal to do with the delicate mood of these films; you almost want to hold your breath during the quiet scenes, without a comforting overlay of music to rely on.)

The scene fades to black, and then comes up on an unusual series of shots: A close-up of a framed photograph of Henry, a candle burning next to it; close-up of a maid, opening a door and announcing the arrival of Victor; an abrupt cut, from the same angle, to a close-up of Victor entering the room; and a close-up of Elizabeth, rising from her chair. Only then do we cut to a wide shot of the enormous room (at the Frankenstein home, it turns out), which would ordinarily be the establishing shot of such a scene.

Whale explained that he opened the sequence this way precisely because it was the opposite of the customary approach. The odd stutter-stepping of the scene's beginning is another indication of the way Whale *sees* cinematically: the rapid collision of large close-ups of heads suggests that Whale had watched some Sergei Eisenstein films (as had most Hollywood filmmakers at the time) as well as *The Cabinet of Dr. Caligari* in preparation for *Frankenstein*. Throughout the expositional scene that unfolds, Whale keeps Henry in the scene by including the photograph – the candle fetishistically arranged next to it – of Henry in various shots (at one point the photo is literally between Elizabeth and Victor, as though Henry is exerting his influence from afar).

With all this care given to a relatively unexceptional scene, it is striking that Whale allows the performances of the two actors to be so slack. They are the 'good' characters, the squares, the sustainers of normalcy. Whale can hardly be bothered with them. John Boles, who appeared in a few quality pictures (King Vidor's *Stella Dallas* [1937], for instance), was all jaw and moustache, a handsome man with a shallow screen presence. Mae Clarke had been effective in Whale's *Waterloo Bridge*, but throughout *Frankenstein* she looks and sounds under-rehearsed. It is as though the director lost interest in Elizabeth and Victor, impatient to get back to the more exotic life represented by Frankenstein's experiments – a feeling reflected by generations of movie-watchers ever since.

James Whale had picked *Frankenstein* off a list of 30 projects offered him by Universal. At the time, he explained his choice by pointing out the 'fine pictorial possibilities', and two grand characterisations – by which he presumably meant Frankenstein and the Monster (*New York Times* 1931e: X4). There is no reason to doubt Whale's avowed reasons for the choice any more than it is impossible not to speculate on the unconscious motivations behind it. Certainly two large issues from Whale's biography find voice in his sympathy for the outcast figure of Monster. Those issues are class and sexual orientation. Whale was from the working class, his father a blast-furnaceman; the Whales had a pig-sty in their backyard (Gatiss 1995: 1). Those who knew him later in life found him the picture of a refined, cultivated Englishman, a member in good standing of Hollywood's community of British ex-pats – Gloria Stuart recalled that Whale led proper tea-time breaks at 11 and 4 o'clock every day on the set of *The Old Dark House* (Weaver 2007: 57). Whale worked hard to erase the stink of the pig-sty and the slop on his boots.

Henry Frankenstein comes from wealth, but creates a man who appears to be a peasant, as though the Monster is an expression of Henry's guilt over his privilege. Robin Wood noted the movie's 'pervasive class references', and placed particular emphasis on the Monster's dress: 'Frankenstein *could* have dressed his creature in top hat, white tie and tails, but in fact chose laborer's clothes' (1979: 7–28). (Mel Brooks would of course correct this choice in *Young Frankenstein*.)

As for Whale's homosexuality informing his work, much has been written and speculated on this subject. *Bride of Frankenstein* is an especially busy collection of gay jokes and wishes. Critic Gary Morris has called the film 'a scathing attack on such hetero institutions as marriage and the family' (1998: p. unknown) in which Henry avoids Elizabeth because of his dalliance with the mincing figure of Dr. Septimus Pretorius (one of the great camp performances in movie history by actor Ernest Thesiger), who literally enters the Frankenstein bedroom one night to seduce Henry away from Elizabeth.

This vein of criticism has rich possibilities, and Whale's blatantly gay references in *Bride* certainly invite such a take. Dr. Pretorius is introduced by one character as 'a very queer-looking gentleman', and one cannot argue the point. But the outcast role of the Monster and his abject place in conventional society, including the family cell, is also well beyond the confines of queer theory, as much as he will always have a place there. The Monster's sense of loneliness, his wonder in nature and his fellow creatures, and his anger, allow him to fit neatly in a Romantic tradition, not so far removed from the more refined sorrows of the heroes of Chateaubriand and Goethe (Shelley's Monster actually finds a copy of *The Sorrows of Young Werther* and reads it).

The 1931 film's articulation of the Monster's lost-ness and childlike sense of confusion is still surprising, watching it eighty years after it was made. The Monster, as his image has invaded our culture, is a stalking thing with arms outstretched, looking for a blonde in a clingy dress. To watch the film again – even though in one scene he does menace

The Monster (Boris Karloff) in his Expressionist cell

a blonde in a clingy dress – is to be reminded of the intense sympathy the film has for him. The very *mise-en-scène* builds pity for him. In the scene of Fritz's taunting of the creature, Whale stages the action two different ways. First, we see it through a proscenium frame, the camera set back to reveal the Monster's dungeon-like room. The crazily-angled design of the chamber, and the tilted shadows that fall across it, are straight out of the German Expressionist school. Within this trap, Karloff's Monster moves in a dance of misery, gesturing awkwardly and swaying back and forth like a zoo animal that has begun to go insane from ill treatment and solitude. Fritz enters with a whip and cracks it at the Monster.

Henry interrupts the scene, and when we return to it, Whale switches to an uncharacteristically visceral tactic. Fritz is now lunging at the Monster with a torch, and Whale switches from the proscenium view to a closer shot of the Monster, cowering against a wall. Cut to an actual point-of-view shot

One of the cinema's great entrances: The Monster (Boris Karloff) fully revealed

from the Monster's position, a close shot of Fritz waving his torch directly at the camera. In this burst of violence, we are the Monster, feeling the heat. (Fritz's death is left off-screen – a blood-curdling scream doing the job – so the sight of the Monster-as-killer does not imprint itself on our brains.)

We have already been disarmed by the Monster in his first proper appearance. As Henry and Waldman are having their 'Have you never wanted to do anything that was dangerous?' conversation, they are silenced by the strange sounds coming from a castle hallway. The Monster is about to back into the room, and into world culture – we are not sure why he actually moves backward through a doorway at this point, but it's a dandy *coup de théâtre* just the same. (Henry turns out the lights in the room when he hears the Monster approach, as though preparing for the star's entrance.) After allowing the looming figure, seen from a distance, to ease into the room, Whale cuts to a medium close-up of the Monster's back and shoulders, and lets him slowly turn around, a neck bolt now curving into view, the light now falling across the hideous face. A cut to a close-up and then an extreme close-up allow the viewer to see the full detail of Jack Pierce's make-up job, but only for a few moments.

It is enough. And those close-ups are as truly black and white as any shots of the 1930s. Henry may have turned the lights off, but some source is rendering the Monster's face as white as the Arctic, his hair black as Hades. Artful shadows spare us the full physiognomic impact, yet these increase the troubled nature of the face. Only the eyes are not vivid and present; the lids half-closed, they are mostly hidden from view, waiting to see and be seen, as a newborn's eyes are not yet ready to fix on an object.

As repulsed as the viewer might be by the Monster's physical deformity, the scene that follows evokes not fear but pity. As though setting a stage, Frankenstein leads the Monster to a chair and bids him sit. A vertiginous shot looks up at Henry and to the skylight as he yanks the pulley that will draw back the window. Karloff has one of his definitive set-pieces in the shots that follow: the Monster rises and gazes upward at the light, then stretches his arms above his body as though trying to grasp the light. (We might remember Henry's words about wanting to know 'what changes a darkness into light', and conjecture whether the 'son' has inherited a similar sense of wonder.) Without cutting away to the skylight again, we know the window slides closed, because the shadow again falls over the Monster's figure. His stitched-up hands are now held out before him, towards Henry, with a peculiar vacant pleading. The camera falls from a close-up of his confused face to a close-up of Karloff's beautiful hands, still gesticulating a question.

QUITE A GOOD SCENE, ISN'T IT?

In looking at the directorial dynamism of these early sequences, it is easy to make the case of *Frankenstein* as a director's film. It makes it even easier when the movie is about an *auteur* who creates his own masterpiece (although in this story the masterpiece rises up to thwart its creator – which, metaphorically speaking, applies to Whale only if you consider that the director was pegged as a maker of horror movies ever after). Henry's musings about wanting to look beyond the clouds and the stars are the wishes of an artist as well as a scientist, and what film director cannot identify with Henry's elated cry, 'Now I know what it feels like to be God!'?

Frankenstein is also an expression of its studio, of the industrial *gestalt* of Universal in the 1930s. It connects with other Universal pictures as a work of art direction, casting, and tendency toward the lurid. The Mittel-European setting was consistent with the Laemmle family's frequent focus on their former homeland, and the crew was stocked with European talents. Much of *Frankenstein*'s cult appeal lies in the way it shares these elements with other Universal horror pictures, which (even before they literally began crossing into each other's turf with the likes of *Frankenstein Meets the Wolf Man*) seem to inhabit a shared cosmos – something that does not cross over with, say, the slightly glossier horror efforts from MGM, even if they starred Karloff (*The Mask of Fu Manchu* [1935]) or Lugosi (*Mark of the Vampire*).

In *The Genius of the System* Thomas Schatz makes a case for Universal's success in the depths of the Depression: the Laemmles stuck to a low-budget approach (despite the A-picture aberration of *All Quiet on the Western Front*), and the horror film fit perfectly into the budget-conscious business plan. Sets could be shrouded in shadow and thus cheapness disguised; monsters were more important than highly-paid stars; and European technicians were already adept at the style (1988: 87–8). *Frankenstein* is one of the films that established the Universal house style under Carl Laemmle, Jr., and the triumph of creativity over budget restrictions is visible throughout…even if the wrinkles in the scrim are visible. (And even if you recognise the leftover town square from *All Quiet on the Western Front*.)

The studio's strengths blossom spectacularly in *Frankenstein*'s coming-to-life scene, the movie's knock-your-socks-off centerpiece. As we have previously noted, Whale said, 'I consider the creation of the monster to be the high spot of the film, because if the audience did not believe the thing had been really made, they would not be bothered with what it was supposed to do afterward' (*New York Times* 1931e: X4). The mechanical part of the sequence is indeed a marvel, with Kenneth Strickfaden's hellzapoppin' buzzers and widgets sparking away and the set rising into its dizzying cylinder of space, a brick-and-mortar birth canal through which the newborn will pass.

The creation itself, to which Whale and Edeson brought their study of *Caligari* and Paul Leni's films, is effective in large part because of the build-up to the event – the long sequence actually begins with a considerable amount of stage-setting. It opens on a miniature exterior of the Frankenstein lab, which rises from a rocky spur amidst a nighttime storm, resembling a Gustave Doré drawing. It is a strange 'castle', if it ever was a castle; it looks more like the remnant of something larger, like the ruined St. Michael's Tower on Glastonbury Tor. Elsewhere Henry's father babbles about his son 'messing around in an old ruined windmill,' evidently a phrase left over from a previous script in which the lab was indeed in the mill – the mill still pressed into service for the movie's finale. (Describing the creation scene, Whale told a journalist, 'Frankenstein puts the spectators in their positions….He is now in a state of feverish excitement, calculated to carry both the spectators in the windmill and the spectators in the theater with him.' So it may be another windmill entirely [*New York Times* 1931e: X4].) The confusion is perhaps apt, since Henry's lab seems to exist only in the realm of fairy tale.

The first shots in the lab show us the amazing height of the set, and they also remind us of Henry's harsh treatment of Fritz, who galumphs around atop the edifice and then shimmies down a rope ladder. Fritz is once again frightened in a childlike way, this time by the storm – another pre-cog sense of his own death. 'You fool,' says Henry, 'if this storm develops as I hope, you'll have plenty to be afraid of before the night's over,' an example of the periodic way Henry seems to address the audience as well as Fritz.

Let us pause for a moment to consider poor Fritz. He is memorably embodied by Dwight Frye, an actor who resembles Universal honcho Carl Laemmle, Jr. in certain photographs. Frye, who died at age 44, gave one of the great performances in the horror genre as Renfield in *Dracula*, and appeared in four *Frankenstein* sequels in various small parts. Theatrical and physical, Frye appeared incapable of dimming his hot-burning light, which might have made him difficult to cast outside the horror game. We know nothing about Fritz, except that he is oddly eager, easily spooked, and perpetually ill-treated by Henry. The bad parenting skills that will surface with Henry's treatment of the Monster are already present in his relationship with his humpbacked assistant. Fritz might have been a previous experiment, a dry run for the Monster, ill-shapen and outcast as he is, but the deck is stacked against him: the Monster has the benefit of rising toward the sky, but Fritz is dwarfish and bent over, a Caliban who does not live long enough to get his own soliloquy.

If the house style of a penny-pinching studio such as Universal included squeezing every dollar out of a set, then

Frankenstein (Colin Clive) informs Waldman (Edward Van Sloan) of
the nature of his experiment

the lab is thoroughly exploited in *Frankenstein*. We really get
to know the interior of that space, especially in a marvelously
fluid shot that follows Henry and Fritz from barred window all
the way across the room to the top of the staircase and back
into the main room, when the secret experimenters are inter-
rupted by a knocking at the castle door. We then see Fritz on
the dark-lit staircase, a mad interior that towers off into an
Expressionist void.

The people at the door are, of course, Elizabeth, Victor and
Dr. Waldman, who *would* show up, unwanted party guests, just
minutes before the blessed event. Henry – this is becoming a
running theme with him – once again tells people to sit 'down,
down!' as he prepares his experiment. He sits Waldman into
the chair in which the Monster will later sink, and delivers a
somewhat taunting introduction to his former teacher while
leaning over him, another example of Frankenstein needing 'to

Frankenstein (Colin Clive) prepares his audience for 'quite a good scene': (l. to r.) Dwight Frye, Edward Van Sloan, John Boles, Mae Clarke

make himself bigger by forcing others down. (For the third time in the scene, he mentions making the creature 'with my own hands', an obsessive tic suggesting both hubris and guilt.) A diagonal spray of moonlight, coming in through a barred window, plays against the back wall as though light is pouring straight out of Henry's fevered head. He then invites the crowd to take a peek at his not-dead, not-yet-alive creature.

Cut to an angle from behind the operating table back towards the group, as Waldman sidles up to view the creature and the others rise. The shot is typical of the film's generally elegant camera sense – it allows us to watch the faces of everybody in the room, with nothing so vulgar as separate close-ups for reactions. Henry then shoos Waldman away, and turns to the crowd, as we cut to him leaning against the gurney. As James Whale put it in a note to Colin Clive upon presenting the script to him, 'In the first scene in his [Frankenstein's] laboratory he becomes very conscious of the theatrical drama and goes a little insane about it' (*New York Times* 1931c: X5). 'Quite a good scene, isn't it?' Henry says. 'One man "crazy", three very sane spectators.' (Of course he leaves out Fritz.) The comment is inspired by Victor's questioning his sanity, but the moment crystallises the theatrical metaphor that runs beneath the film's storyline, the idea of Frankenstein as a mad artist who pulls levers, fixes lights, directs the other actors and creates something never seen before.

The stage having been set, what follows is pure theatre. But it also looks like science – there is enough attention lavished on the machines and enough vague medical talk from Frankenstein and Waldman to make it credible. Yes, the lightning storm is a Gothic touch (no such electrical boost was needed in Shelley's novel, where the creation is left off stage), but all those meters and pulleys do make it look as though the damned thing might actually *work*. Thus *Frankenstein* is not a supernatural film, but a scientific one, no matter how far-fetched. Vampire pictures clearly operate in another realm, but in the world of *Frankenstein* there is always the possibility these things might happen.

In its machinery and its emphasis on science, *Frankenstein* fits the mood of 1931. Post-Industrial Revolution but pre-Space Age, the film can catch the excitement of Frankenstein imagining a new world with power over death, but can also dread the results of that experiment, in which the creation goes out of the creator's control. The metaphor of the Frankenstein Monster has been handily employed for everything from Germany's elevation of Hitler to the development of the atomic bomb. But in *Frankenstein*, science itself is not the culprit. There is no actual equivalent of the familiar speech from many a mad scientist film to follow, the 'there are things man was not meant to meddle in' conclusion, even if Waldman is around to tut-tut the project. The experiment worked; it was the human element that failed – Fritz's cruelty, Waldman's scepticism, Frankenstein's inability to nurture his progeny.

In 1931, a glance at the newspapers would confirm that global systems were broken. The fantasy of a civilised Europe had been smashed by the slaughterhouse of World War I, the model of capitalism had bankrupted the West, and the model of communism was starving to death in the Soviet Union. Into this world stalked Frankenstein's Monster, the embodiment of the highest man-made ambitions the world could offer. And it goes on a blind, terrified rampage. Audiences responded to this scenario with enthralled raptness, as though their worst suspicions about How Things Worked were being played out on the screen, in the way genre pictures can distill the temper of the times.

But the creation sequence narrows its focus from the grand machinery to the close-up of a human – very human – hand. The Monster stirs to life. The quivering of the hand sends Henry into a paroxysm of triumph, the others having to hold him down as he shouts, 'It's alive!' and 'Now I know what it feels like to *be* God!' These few seconds lead us to a couple of cult truisms: Two measurements of a cult movie are A) its ability to sanctify lines of dialogue into the vernacular, and B) its underground credibility as something that has been censored or suppressed. The censorship issues were mentioned in Chapter Two, with Henry's 'God' moment one of the lines that vanished from the picture for many years (and the Monster's disturbing encounter with the little girl a visual jolt that got snipped). 'It's alive!', especially in the last 30 years, has been a catchphrase for all manner of pop media: the title of a Ramones live album and a Larry Cohen evil baby movie, a sample for rap musicians, and a slot at #49 on the American Film Institute's list of greatest movie quotes.

In this eruption it is easy to see how Colin Clive has about him the air of a fanatical saint – the bony thinness, the utter certainty of cause, the striving for ecstasy that strongly suggests a sexual urge sublimated into his vocation. Clive is skinny but big-boned, in the manner of Anthony Perkins; he has the huge, tortured features of a monk. His horsiness fits the high-strung nature of the character, and corresponds to Whale's conception of Henry: 'Frankenstein's nerves are all to pieces. He is a very strong, extremely dominant personality, sometimes quite strange and queer, sometimes very soft, sympathetic and decidedly romantic' (*New York Times* 1931c: X5).

At the climax of the creation sequence, the screen fades to black, Henry's laughter still audible. This has arguably been the high point of the movie, and when it ends (at the film's 25-minute mark) one might forgive a certain dropping-off of intensity. *Frankenstein*, however, keeps barrelling right along, with almost no dead patches for the remainder of its running time. After the intro of Baron Frankenstein and the much-needed philosophical break with Henry and Waldman, we rush through the unveiling of the Monster, the death of Fritz, and the 'rescue' of Henry by his father with Elizabeth and Victor. Henry collapses after scuffling with the Monster, and his loved ones spirit him away from his lab.

Waldman stays behind to preserve Henry's records and 'painlessly destroy' the Monster. This upholder of all that is moral gives the Monster some sort of lethal injection and writes in a notebook that he is about to dissect the body, *which is not yet dead*. Has any viewer ever hoped Waldman will succeed? Whale tracks most of this from a superbly-chosen angle above the action, from approximately where a student would be looking down upon a surgical theatre. A cutaway to the Monster's face lets us know he is still alive, his eyes fluttering. Waldman rolls out a tray of scalpels and other instruments, turning his back on the Monster, and his movement in getting the tray forces the camera to accommodate him, thus leaving the Monster out of the shot – and allowing the viewer a few tense moments of imagining that the creature must surely be rising from his gurney. Waldman turns back to the table and no, the Monster is still there, immobile. As Waldman wedges himself in between the Monster's torso and a languidly outstretched arm, he seals his fate – for (without a cut to hype the moment) the Monster slowly raises the arm and clutches his hand around Waldman's neck. And that is how a horror scene is directed.

In the brief scene that follows, we see the Monster by himself, stalking about the staircase and the entryway and then out the door. It is a strange interlude; the Monster is alone and free for the first time, and at this moment he changes from being acted upon to driving the action. And yet he is not onscreen much from here. We quickly move from the active Monster to the passive Henry, in one of the movie's strangest scenes: Henry sits in a chair, presumably on the Frankenstein estate, with Elizabeth seated on the ground by

After the experiment: Henry (Colin Clive) and Elizabeth (Mae Clarke) relaxing at home

his side. They are on what appears to be an elevated porch extending into the trees. Elegantly dressed yet with the air of a patient coming out of a luxury detox facility, Henry looks like a languid Jazz Age refugee from an F. Scott Fitzgerald story. There is even a greyhound lounging at his feet. The setting is all draped tree limbs and dappled sun, the mood is utter collapse.

Gone is Henry's fire, although he alludes, perhaps with residual excitement, to the 'horrible' days and nights spent in pursuit of his creation. But he has promised Elizabeth he will not think of those things anymore – bad thoughts must be quashed. Mere days earlier he had been transcending the need for God, and vanquishing the tyranny of death. He tells her it is heaven being there with her, and she reminds him that heaven was not far away all the time.

Given the language, and Whale's sly humour, it is not too hard to infer that this vision of 'heaven' is truly the end of life – a dreary, washed-out existence with no untidy thoughts and no electrifying experiments to distract one from the placidity of home and hearth. (In most *Frankenstein* films that followed – even at the chintzy level of *I Was a Teenage Frankenstein* – the pattern of the scientist being tugged away from his work by a nattering fiancée or wife is consistent. This is a rich irony for something based on a novel by a woman. In fact, part of the appeal of *Frankenstein* for adolescent boys of all ages is surely the theme of not wanting to grow up and settle down just yet.) In this tableau, Henry resembles nothing so much as the drained male victim of a female succubus from a late 19th-century painting – but in this case the woman is not a femme fatale, but the bland face of domesticity.

The sole narrative thread for the remainder of the picture is the wedding of Henry and Elizabeth – in fact, most of what follows occurs on the single day of the wedding: the street party of the townspeople, the Monster's encounter with the little girl, his arrival at the Frankenstein home to menace Elizabeth and the final great hunt. As the wedding day shapes up, the film finds opportunities to tease Baron Frankenstein's overt class snobbery, something Whale must have relished. An awareness of class and a tweaking of the rich was a commonplace trope for early 1930s Hollywood cinema, and *Frankenstein* participates to some extent – yet it is true that we laugh *with* the Baron, not merely at him, a conflict that might reflect Whale's own infatuation with status.

The Baron fobs off cheap champagne on the servants, noting that the fine wine is wasted on them, and is condescending to the Bavarian villagers who are essentially his vassals, calling them 'boys and girls' and pompously allowing himself to be seen by them. Again we return to the idea that the film is a series of power struggles among people eager to assert their will over someone, or some*thing*, else; 'It's extraordinary how friendly you can make people on a couple of bottles of beer,' he says of the locals, who are gathering like happy Bavarian Munchkins beneath his window. 'Tomorrow they'll all be fighting.' His view of human capabilities is as deterministic as Dr. Waldman's.

Frederick Kerr's broad performance notwithstanding, there is something vaguely sinister about the Baron. His pronouncements invariably endorse the bourgeois status quo, and again that line of Henry's – 'My father doesn't believe in anyone' – lingers. When the Baron chortles about his grandfather having been forbidden to drink by his grandmother, it is another subtle dig at marriage as an institution.

He is also oddly prescient in telling Henry 'I hope in thirty years' time a youngster of yours will be carrying on the tradition'; he means giving the Frankenstein bridal veil to a wife, but the prediction might as well refer to the family legacy of experimenting with dead human parts. There is a peculiar cutaway to Henry after the Baron toasts (as the elder

Frankenstein will in the film's final moments, using slightly different wording) 'a son of the house of Frankenstein', as a boyish, inward-directed smile plays across Henry's face. Is this standard sheepishness, or is Henry thinking about the 'son' he has already begotten?

TWISTED ANY WAY

If *Frankenstein* were merely a well-plotted tale well told, it might be highly regarded, but not a classic. In fact, the narrative is problematic at times, with its share of internal inconsistencies and a few puzzling developments, the kind of things that keep online message boards humming on classic horror movie sites. But the film actually succeeds more on the level of dream than it does as a narrative, and surely that is the source of its staying power. Henry is the dreamer, and the sequence with Elizabeth and the sleeping greyhound might be the interlude of waking, before the re-arrival of the Monster confirms that the nightmare is in control.

Whale's fluency within scenes is usually spot-on, but the transitions are often eccentric – a peculiar quality that actually enhances the film's fantastic effect. (In a similar way, although Tod Browning's film of *Dracula* is casually downgraded as a creaky, antique adaptation of a play, surely part of its unsettling impact comes from its weird rhythms, druggy line readings and oppressive interiors.) One of *Frankenstein*'s most dreamlike transitions comes at the end of a shot (actually one of Whale and Edeson's more bravura efforts) of the townspeople partying in the streets, a travelling shot that passes through various groups of whirling dancers in traditional dress. The shot begins to dissolve as the camera tracks along a diagonal line of people; it is replaced by a shot moving in a similar fashion, this time along a diagonal line of trees. Within those trees we see the Monster, thrashing along before us. It is an uncanny moment for a number of reasons: the contrast of community and loneliness is sharp, and the dropping off of blaring music into the near-silence of the Monster's walk is worthy of Kurosawa as an aural dynamic.

What follows is the Monster's encounter with Maria, the little girl who ends up vanishing into the lake, which has been previously discussed. Having not intended to hurt the girl, why does the Monster show up at Elizabeth's bedroom window, clearly intending mischief? This point has bothered various *Frankenstein* commentators over the years, especially given that the Monster has elicited great sympathy up to this point. If we play with the idea that the Monster is a dream-projection of Henry's, a creature who might function with a freedom Henry is being denied, then his arrival at the bed-room window makes perfect sense – he is trying to stop the wedding. If *Frankenstein* is a fable about growing up, then it fits into a longstanding narrative tradition that, for Hollywood, stretches from *The Birth of a Nation* to *Brokeback Mountain*: it is about yearning to remain in freedom, in a fantasy of youth.

A stray detail (but one that merits its own close-up) has Henry locking Elizabeth in her bedroom as he and Victor go searching for the intruder. Nothing overtly suggests Henry's collusion with the Monster's mission; we have seen him lock people in a room before, when the visitors arrived just as the lightning storm settled in over the experiment. Maybe he is just a control freak. Or maybe he *wants* the Monster to disrupt the wedding.

If the Monster's stalking of Elizabeth is enigmatic, so is his departure without completing his job. We go from the interior of the bedroom (where, in a set-up appropriated from *The Cabinet of Dr. Caligari*, Whale has skillfully wrenched suspense from having the Monster climb in the window in the background of a shot occupied by Elizabeth in the foreground), to

The Monster (Boris Karloff) leaves Elizabeth (Mae Clarke) in imitation of Fuseli's *Nightmare* composition

Henry and Victor in the basement, where they hear Elizabeth's screams. When we return to the room, the bride is draped across the bed in an allusion to the famous 1781 painting 'The Nightmare', by Henry Fuseli – but it's also a direct image from Mary Shelley (who herself might have used the Fuseli painting as a reference): 'She was there, lifeless and inanimate, thrown across the bed, her head hanging down and her pale and distorted features half covered by her hair' (1981: 179). We glimpse the Monster sneaking away from the window. What did he do? Did he feel more compassion, in the end, than Frankenstein, or simply run at the threat of exposure?

Hard to tell, because we never see Elizabeth again (except, supposedly, in the distance in the final shot, in the coda not filmed by Whale). Henry's farewell to Victor is marked by a sense of Henry's own imminent death, as though he knows he will not survive without his double; the movie clearly sets up Victor as the custodian of Elizabeth's future (visually speaking, it has frequently paired him with her). This is preparing the original ending of the picture, with Henry dead along with the Monster, the ending that Universal junked when test audiences disapproved.

The linkage of Henry with the Monster is repeated during the chase sequence (a sequence that, among other things, gave the spectacle of angry villagers with torches to countless horror films that followed). The patently soundstagey mountain set fulfills the movie's visual scheme of Expressionist angles – this world, from the opening sequence, has been tilted and askew, the logic of nightmare and fairy tale holding sway. When Henry finds the Monster, or vice versa, Whale takes time for a rhythmic series of four close-ups of them holding each other's gaze, an ambiguous and charged moment in which the two men are equally matched. They scuffle; Henry is knocked out. Now, if the Monster is intent on killing his father/God, he might do so here. Instead, hearing the sounds of the angry villagers, he picks up Henry's body and takes it to an old mill… thus unconsciously mimicking Henry's own process in making a life. But the Monster's will to power can extend only to taking away life, not creating it. He did not get the genius brain, after all. The only power he can exercise is to kill Henry, which, by all the evidence, he wants to do in the windmill.

There they share the looking-through-the-gears moment of union; adding to the confusion, a villager shouts, 'There he is! The murderer!' as the two men stand on the parapet of the windmill – but is he talking about the Monster, or the scientist? After the Monster flings Henry from the mill, the villagers burn the structure down. As if there were any doubt about the film's sympathies at this point, Whale shows the villagers as a virtual lynch mob, while the Monster moans and howls at the top of the mill, baying like an animal in a trap. This scapegoating of the outsider, the hounding of the dark Other by an illegal mob, has a curious forcefulness that seems to go beyond the story (and has no correlative in Shelley's novel). It predicts the anti-lynching pictures that Hollywood would offer in the near future, most famously Fritz Lang's *Fury* (1936) and William Wellman's *The Ox-Bow Incident* (1943). More hauntingly, one cannot help but note that knowledge of the pogroms against Jews would be still alive in the minds of the European *émigrés* who collaborated on the film, or that 1931 was a time when the lynching of black people was still a reality in America. As the 1930s developed, the hatred of racial and religious minorities would reach unprecedented savagery in the world; that kind of dread frequently expresses itself in popular culture, and it seems to raise its head here.

As for Whale, he adopted a breezy, I've-got-a-greyhound-sitting-at-my-slippered-feet air in speaking of the finale. 'The villagers were thrown in for nothing,' he said a month after the film's opening, 'merely as a background for the blood-hounds, whose yowls formed such a delightful background to the pagan sport of a mountain man-hunt' (*New York Times* 1931e: X4). One assumes a languid pause there for an arched eyebrow and a long draw on a cigarette. But remember that Whale spent much of his life adopting a persona for himself, and compare this jolly flippancy with the intensity of the movie sequence as it plays out – Karloff's ape-like beating at the railings, the torch-lit close-ups of shrieking villagers – and Whale's attitude doesn't scan.

As originally shot, Henry Frankenstein and his creation would die together at the mill. For reasons explained in Chapter Two, the ending was scrapped and a new final scene added to allow Henry to survive. Commenting on the change, James Whale said, 'The semi-happy ending was added to remind the audience that after all it is only a tale that is told, and could easily be twisted any way by the director.' (This is an unusual comment, practically pre-postmodern, the kind of thing Abbas Kiarostami might have said of the ending of *Taste of Cherry* [1997].) The ending – a single shot – consists of the household maids bringing the marriage wine to the door of the room where Henry is recuperating. Their knock is answered by Baron Frankenstein, with Henry in bed in the background, tended by Elizabeth.

Although the scene is an add-on, made without Whale or Clive, it is intriguing. The Baron, after referring to the fact that this is the same wine his grandmother forbade his grandfather to drink, begins to take a glass back to Henry, then stops himself. 'Mr. Henry doesn't need this,' he says, reaching over and closing the door to the room. The implicit leer is a familiar Hollywood wink-nudge: ah, the amorous couple in the bridal chamber! At this point, we cannot be sure how long Henry has been recovering, or whether Henry and Elizabeth have been married. (*Bride of Frankenstein* opens in the immediate aftermath of the events of the first film, and the couple is definitely not married.)

And so the Baron raises the glass and repeats his toast from earlier in the film: 'Here's to a son to the house of Frankenstein.' The maids are titillated by the sexual suggestion, and the moment is surely meant as a way to get offstage and bring the curtain down. Yet the casual comment brings us back to the movie's obsession with the creation of life, and how far Henry has retreated from his larger ambitions. (*Frankenstein* thus joins an interesting list of movies with endings, compromised by studio interference, that feel stranger and more disturbing than the intended dark ending: Hitchcock's *Suspicion* (1941), for instance, which instead of killing off Cary Grant at the end, leaves suspicious wife Joan Fontaine to live with her untrustworthy husband for the rest of her life, or Lang's *Woman in the Window* (1944), where the final revelation solves the protagonist's problems but opens up another intriguing realm of creepy suggestion about his character.)

Even more important than Henry's survival is that the Monster, ostensibly dead at the end of *Frankenstein*, is also alive, available to return in *Bride of Frankenstein* and the sequels. Nothing in the movie itself hints at this; we see the creature collapse inside the burning windmill, clocked on the head and evidently pinned by a falling beam. But if there is any principle to come from the Universal horror films, it is this: there is always a way to survive the direst calamity; there is always a pool of water in the basement of the burning windmill. To a child watching the Universal classics, these repeated resurrections are an important revelation. They mean that a movie's narrative integrity is an untrustworthy thing, that forces outside the film could change the meaning of what you had seen.

And the ending of *Frankenstein* could only carry its original meaning for viewers until the release of *Bride of Frankenstein*. For the rest of us, Baron Frankenstein's twinkling joke and the final reassurance of Henry and Elizabeth cosying up together is merely a temporary finger in the dike. *Frankenstein* is a 71-minute film, entire unto itself; but it is not, either. It is a porous, flexible work, containing the seeds of future iterations and retroactively changed by the movies to come. The ending of *Frankenstein* can never be rounded off, because as the door closes on Henry and Elizabeth and the Baron downs his glass of wine, a larger story is beginning.

5

THE MONSTER'S PLACE

Set just after the Spanish Civil War, Victor Erice's *The Spirit of the Beehive* (1973) is one of the essential films about childhood. The film's small town is visited by a travelling picture-show man, who sets up his projector in a school house and presents the original *Frankenstein* to the enthralled locals. *Spirit*'s central character, seven-year-old Ana (played by the uncanny Ana Torrent), is deeply affected by the movie, which haunts her through the rest of the film – there is even a sequence that echoes the Monster-with-the-little-girl scene from *Frankenstein*, as Ana's imagination conjures this scary/comforting figure.

Erice's film was a reminder of that figure's elemental power. By 1973, the Monster had been appropriated for cartoons, cereal boxes, and TV sitcoms and Mel Brooks would have his way with the myth within a year. *The Spirit of the Beehive* was a welcome summoning of the original demon of *Frankenstein*, a return to the beginnings of that image's ability to stride darkly into our dreams, waking or otherwise. Having travelled through the pop-culture Cuisinart, the Monster still loomed large.

Today, Frankenstein remains a force, in ways that could not have been imagined in 1931, or even 1973. As the first decade of the 21st century closed, the image of the Monster continued to be visible in everyday life. In 2007, a made-in-China plastic tumbler designed in the form of the Monster's face was recalled by its manufacturer for containing lead. (Still a threat after all these years.) Mel Brooks's Broadway musical based on *Young Frankenstein* opened to strong business. Children's book author Adam Rex published *Frankenstein Makes a Sandwich*, launching the adventures of the Monster as a picture-book hero. In 2011 the Oscar-winning director Danny Boyle mounted a blockbuster stage production of *Frankenstein*, re-igniting a pop-culture phenomenon. A restaurant in Michigan introduced the Frankenstein Burger, a seven-pound behemoth that was free to any customer who could actually eat it in an hour. And US senator and 2008 presidential candidate John McCain developed a frequently-used one-liner to deflect questions about his age, proudly declaring, 'I'm older than dirt and have more scars than Frankenstein' (Sisk 2008). (As ever, the names of scientist and creation are casually transposed.)

In short, the 1931 film known as *Frankenstein* (more so than Mary Shelley's novel, or any stage adaptation, or any sequel/spin-off) has contributed an image to world culture that is familiar even to people who have never seen the film. The process by which something disreputable becomes something mainstream is a complicated one, and the 80-years-plus timeline of *Frankenstein* gives us a large history with which to work. (One is tempted to quote the John Huston character in *Chinatown* (1974), and conclude that 'Politicians, ugly buildings and whores all get respectable if they last long enough,' but *Frankenstein* has gone beyond respectability and into the realm of beloved.) *The Spirit of the Beehive* is merely one example of the inspiration the Monster has provided, which manifests itself in unexpected ways. Stan Lee has said that his comic-book creation, the Hulk, was partly inspired by the Frankenstein monster, claiming, '(I)t seemed to me that the monster, played by Boris Karloff, wasn't really a bad guy. He was the good guy. He didn't want to hurt anybody. It's just those idiots with torches kept running up and down the mountains, chasing him and getting him angry' (DeFalco 2003: page unknown). Johnny Cash told *Walk the Line* (2005) director James Mangold his favorite film was *Frankenstein*; the singer sympathised with the Monster, another 'Man in Black' made up of bad parts (Papamichael 2007).

Chronicling the many permutations of the Frankenstein phenomenon in its post-'Shock!' TV phase would take up another book. As the sampling above – gleaned from the simplest of Google searches – suggests, the Monster has expressed himself in nearly every form imaginable. (Susan Tyler Hitchcock's 2007 book *Frankenstein: A Cultural History* – the existence of which itself is proof of the viability of the Frankenstein brand name – does a far-reaching job of cataloguing such ephemera.) A few of these are worth detailing, especially for the things they imply about how a cult might mutate into different forms.

Comic books, for instance, have long played with the Monster as a character, but not always as the incarnation of fear. He was re-cast as a superhero (complete with tights and bulging biceps) in a mid-1960s run, not the first or last time the Monster would shift from a menacing figure (however sympathetic and abused he might have been in the 1931 film) to a heroic one. It prefigured the way Arnold Schwarzenegger's villain in the original *Terminator* (1984) flipped narrative roles in the sequels of that series. In the 1987 film *The Monster Squad*, the Universal baddies banded together to make mischief and were battled by a pubescent team of monster-slayers; but the Frankenstein monster ends up switching sides and cud-

The Monster's image has appeared everywhere, including the head of a PEZ dispenser (photo: Evyan Horton)

dling a teddy bear. The stop-motion puppet film *Mad Monster Party* (1969), with Karloff doing the voice of 'Baron Boris von Frankenstein', gave the kiddie version of the cute monsters reuniting. Whether his head was used to top a PEZ dispenser or dangle from a key chain, the Monster was absorbed into a catchy, non-terrifying twentieth-century iconography.

Any lingering doubt about the Monster's respectability ended in 1997. In a series of postage stamps called 'Tales and Legends', a sketch of Mary Shelley's creature stared out of a UK stamp; in 2008, in celebrating two British film power-houses (the *Carry On* series and Hammer Films), the poster for *The Curse of Frankenstein* was included in a set of six stamps. 1997 was also the year the US postal service issued its 'Classic Movie Monsters' set, five different images: Karloff as the Monster and the Mummy, Bela Lugosi as Dracula, Lon Chaney as The Phantom of the Opera and Lon Chaney, Jr., as the Wolf Man. Karloff made it again in 2002, when the US issued a 'Behind the Scenes' tribute to the film industry that included the actor sitting for his *Frankenstein* make-up.

And yet, however much the Monster and his maker might have been taken up by the mainstream, they remain alive and at play in the subculture. The persistence of the Monster's image in the annals of rock and roll, for instance, hints at the usefulness of the icon as a counterculture badge. Edgar Winter's heavier-than-thou 1973 guitar-synth instrumental was called 'Frankenstein', he said, because the finished track was stitched together out of different pieces of tape, although the sonic attack of the song is truly a monster. (Winter suffers from albinism, which might lend further subtext to his appropriation of the Monster.) There have been rock groups called Karloff (out of Göteborg, Sweden) and Electric Frankenstein (New Jersey) and at least a half-dozen entities called Frankenstein. South Carolina rock combo Mary Shelley Overdrive uses Universal Horror imagery on their 2008 release, 'Bride of Shock Theatre', Alice Cooper penned a tune, misspelled but oddly sincere, called 'The Ballad of Dwight Fry,' and the New York Dolls – whose lead singer, David Johansen, has a distinctly Frankensteinian facial structure – had a punk anthem called 'Frankenstein', one of the best of the many songs by that title. And few songs have charted as often as the novelty tune 'Monster Mash', originally released in 1962, a genuinely clever ode to the major monsters performed in unmistakably Karloffian mimicry by Bobby 'Boris' Pickett.

The fact that a punk band in 2013 calls itself Electric Frankenstein ('the most hard-working underground rock band of the last twenty years' as per their website) defies a certain subcultural logic – is not the subculture all about adopting new images, rejecting the status quo? Is not the Frankenstein mythos a little, well, *old*? And yet, despite his place in advertising and harmless kiddie fare, the Monster retains his appeal in the subculture – surely because he is the rejected one, the outcast figure unredeemed by pop-culture visibility.

META FRANKENSTEIN

I suggested in Chapter 3 that the opening sequence in *Bride of Frankenstein* was the moment the Frankenstein myth turned self-conscious: its depiction of Mary and Percy Shelley parrying quips with Lord Byron at the Villa Diodati became an opportunity for the phenomenon to comment on itself. In that fanciful prologue, the principals were actually talking about the aftermath of the writing and publishing of *Frankenstein*. Three films made in a weirdly short time (1986-1990) re-imagine the original summer of 1816, and the stormy elements that gave birth to Mary's literary creation. The first out of the gate, and the loudest, was Ken Russell's *Gothic* (1986), an over-the-top orgy in which a monster roams the Villa. Its baldly stated thesis is that the free-thinkers' artistic imaginations are responsible for manifesting Something Awful in the house. Ivan Passer's *Haunted Summer* (1988), based on a novel by Anne Edwards, takes a youthful approach to the idyll, with Byron as a controlling Dr. Frankenstein type and Mary as a pre-feminist who sees through his manipulations. Roger Corman's *Frankenstein Unbound* (1990), from a Brian Aldiss novel, has a pulpier feel than the other tellings, yet its central idea is much more interesting: a 21st-century scientist time-trips back to 1816, and discovers there was a real Victor Frankenstein, upon whom Mary Shelley based her supposedly fictional work.

Another of *Frankenstein*'s creators was celebrated and fictionalised in *Gods and Monsters* (1998), written and directed by Bill Condon from Christopher Bram's novel *Father of Frankenstein*. Financially secure and long retired from Hollywood, the real James Whale committed suicide in his swimming pool on May 29, 1957, the same year his horror pictures were discovered by a new generation of fans. *Gods and Monsters* freely speculates on Whale's final days, in a scenario revolving around the elegantly-appointed but ailing director (Ian McKellen) and his infatuation with a gardener (Brendan Fraser). The imagery of *Frankenstein* is important to the film (Fraser's broad, big-browed head even evokes the Monster), which flashes back to on-set moments in the making of *Bride of Frankenstein*. Implicit in the mix is the idea that Whale is creating another Monster out of unformed clay – perhaps creating a Monster in order to be killed by him.

These shards of the myth have been accompanied by occasional stabs at the Monster story: *The Bride* (1985), with Sting and *Flashdance* (1983) star Jennifer Beals leading the cast, could not escape the taint of MTV about it; Tim Burton's *Frankenweenie* (1984) offered a charming short-form tale of a dog brought back to life by its young owner, whose name happened to be Victor Frankenstein; and in 1994 a big-budget version, the awkwardly-titled *Mary Shelley's Frankenstein*, found life with Kenneth Branagh (who also directed) as the creator and Robert De Niro as the creation. Conceptually, the idea of the director of the movie also playing Frankenstein is interesting, and underlines the theatrical suggestions of Whale's original film, but Branagh's movie proved as bombastic and over-stated as the 1931 film had been trim and subtle.

Television provided a vehicle for re-thinkings, and two vital series of the 1990s-2000s, *Buffy the Vampire Slayer* and *The X-Files*, both featured episodes devoted to fresh versions of the Frankenstein myth. The 1997 *X-Files* episode, puckishly titled 'The Post-Modern Prometheus', is an ambitious, black-and-white, tonally bizarre installment written and directed by series creator Chris Carter. It makes a number of references to the 1931 film, including the line 'It's alive' and a climax involving villagers with torches, although the overall tone is decidedly tongue-in-cheek.

If TV was hip to the power of the original, Universal Pictures could seem befuddled by their endowment. *Van Helsing* (2004) was a special-effects-heavy attempt to revive the old monster gang, with an interesting new design for the Frankenstein monster. But its re-imagining of vampire-hunter Van Helsing as a virile, indestructible young stud was indicative of the generally feather-headed superficiality of the project. By comparison, the 1944 *House of Frankenstein* makes sense. In 2008, an animated film called *Igor* brought another familiar franchise character to protagonist status, as the hunchback assistant was revealed to be a scientific genius in his own right, his talents far outstripping those of his employer, Dr. Glickenstein. The film presumes audience familiarity with the Frankenstein universe, enough to get jokes about the hero attending a mad-scientist's-assistant school where one can secure a 'Yes Master' degree.

Tim Burton returned to his youthful short film and created an animated black-and-white feature-length version of *Frankenweenie*, released in 2012. A mild flurry of Frankenstein projects kicked up: the Monster returned in cartoon form in *Hotel Transylvania* (2012) – a film pitched to young viewers far removed from the mythology of the mad monster party on view (but nevertheless a box-office hit), and *I, Frankenstein* was set for 2014 release.

IT LIVES AGAIN

Like electric bolts administered to keep a body alive, two important advancements kept the world of *Frankenstein* thriving. One was home video, which created a collector's market in old movies and a chance for devotees to closely study a cult picture such as *Frankenstein*; the other was the Internet.

When DVD became the dominant home-entertainment mode, Universal went to some lengths to treat its classic monster movies as crown jewels, debuting deluxe packages in 1999 and box sets in 2004 (the *Frankenstein* box contained the original film as well as four sequels). 2006 brought yet another release, a 75th-anniversary package featuring a new print of the movie and supplemental materials. And even though the days of the repertory theatre began to fade when the video store rose up, 35 mm prints of *Frankenstein* and the other Universal warhorses would still periodically tour big cities, even if just to publicise another new DVD or blu-ray release.

The Internet allowed fans of golden-age horror to connect and confab, or to energetically blog on the subject. In 2007 a Montreal illustrator, Pierre Fournier, launched *Frankensteinia*, a busy and very handsome website collecting all manner of Frankenstein-related news and images. Sites such as *The Vault of Horror* and *Monster Kid Online Magazine* keep the flame of cult-horror worship going, Mary Shelley's novel can be read online at a variety of sources, and academic websites give cultural-history context to the novel and the film. In 2012 *Frankenstein* had two separate Facebook pages, and another Facebook page as a 'Public Figure', thus giving new cyber-meaning to the Monster's plaintive cry: 'Friend?' has become 'Friend me?'

Nowhere is the online chatter more devoted and informed than on the Classic Horror Film Board, a busy meeting place for disciples of all levels of the horror film (the site is divided into a variety of time periods and subgenres, including a section for Universal Horrors). Like medieval religious scholars, the commentators here – who range from amateur buffs to published authors to filmmakers – sift through the tiniest issues within the canon, invariably with wit and passion. A topic posted in October 2005, on the subject 'Frankenstein Meets the Wolf Man', had over eight thousand – *eight thousand* – responses by June 2013, as detailed arguments, bad puns, and thoughtful appreciations of the Frankenstein Monster were/are unpacked one by one.

Younger bloggers have a tendency to view *Frankenstein* as something of a museum piece, something to be respected but not especially excited about. Meanwhile, the message boards at the Internet Movie Database, always a lively arena for pronouncements and debates, are mostly positive. 'Bones729' complained, 'The acting is so ridiculous and overdone, the editing is lame', in decrying the movie's place in IMDb's Top 250 rankings. Even enthusiastic posters have a tendency to apologise for the movie's 'primitive technology' and 'dated' aspects, as though there is some kind of guilt associated with esteeming such an ancient picture. But most carry affection for the movie, which 'Leatherface33' sums up in a typical response: 'I don't know what it is about *Frankenstein*, but I love it... What a kick ass movie.' Nothing has dimmed the film's status at the head of the horror movie table, although when people conduct polls of the greatest horror movies, the results tend to be weighted towards more recent offerings, such as *Psycho* (1960) (according to the American Film Institute), *The Exorcist* (1973) (*Entertainment Weekly*), or *The Texas Chainsaw Massacre* (1974) (*Premiere*).

When such polls are held, the 1931 film often plays second fiddle to its first sequel. *Bride of Frankenstein* is frequently cited as the greater movie, and it is easy to understand the ranking; it has a suppleness that the original film, with its peculiar rhythm and handful of clanking supporting performances, lacks. *Bride of Frankenstein*'s rich humour and brazen sexual insinuations mark it as a more daring picture, and Franz Waxman's score is a treasure.

All of this is valid. Yet – perhaps because of *Bride of Frankenstein*'s cheeky humour – the original film remains

Parody image of the Shepard Fairey HOPE poster of Barack Obama, adapted for the Frankenstein monster by Shane Parker; reproduced with permission of Shane Parker

spookier. The 1931 *Frankenstein* is hardly a polished example of grand studio filmmaking, but a somewhat humpbacked work: the ungainly aural treatment of the early-sound era, the unpredictable editing, the carelessness of some of the line readings. At times in my life when I have re-visited *Frankenstein*, I have been surprised to discover how spare and simple it is, when my memory had blown it up into something more complicated – yet I would argue that this simplicity, which we see on the surface of the 71-minute movie, is key to its richness, in the same way a classic fairy tale, with its every detail tellingly chosen, can devastate in the course of three pages.

Frankenstein's rough edges – and its classification as a horror film – keep it from being entirely absorbed by the respectable culture. Yes, the *image* of the Monster has infiltrated all levels of media, but the movie itself still has its awkwardness, its shambling rhythm. As usual, the Monster, that all-purpose metaphor maker, provides his own allegory: he is forever the rude beast breaking up the civilised wedding party (or, as even more vividly depicted in a memorable sequence in the TV-made *Frankenstein: The True Story*, the hideous creature striding into the fancy ball, disturbing aristocratic society and spilling blood on the floor). When knock-offs of Shepard Fairey's celebrated HOPE poster of presidential candidate Barack Obama began appearing during the 2008 campaign, the monster found his way into one such parody, designed by Shane Parker; the word below the image is FEAR. *Frankenstein*, that midnight strider, is always there to remind us of the dark half, the part that cannot be hidden, the demon that lurks beneath the shell of polite existence. No amount of enshrinement in the pop-culture pantheon can quite smooth out its edges.

In September 2008 Universal announced a multi-picture deal with director Guillermo del Toro, a lifelong *Frankenstein* fan who included excerpts from the 1931 film in his *Hellboy II* (2008). According to the press release, del Toro would make new versions of *Dr. Jekyll and Mr. Hyde*, the Dickens novel *The Mystery of Edwin Drood* (filmed by Universal in 1935), and the big one: *Frankenstein*. Promising neither a faithful adaptation of the Shelley novel or the Whale film, del Toro indicated an interest in his own 'permutation' of the story and in telling the myth in a different way. Yet somehow one assumes the presence of roiling test tubes, a malformed assistant arranging fleshy pieces, and torches. The project stalled, but del Toro announced in October 2012 that he was newly at work on a screenplay (McCabe: 2012). In 2009

Universal talked to *The Illusionist* (2006) director Neil Burger about tackling a remake of *Bride of Frankenstein*, an idea that has kicked around at various times since the ill-fated Sting/Jennifer Beals *Bride*; the project is currently slated for 2015 release. Also slated for 2015 is a Frankenstein film with Igor (played by Daniel Radcliffe) brought to full co-starring status.

And so the Monster and his maker, playing out their drama of self and shadow, of God and Adam, of parent and child, continue to tread. Mary Shelley first set them walking through the forests and mountains of Europe in 1816, and they have stalked across countless painted soundstages since 1931. A story about the creation of life has itself continued to create life, leaving its traces of the uncanny on each generation; in its shadowplay we perceive the outlines of our fears of family rejection, social abjectness, death, and the less controllable parts of our own nature. It's alive, and it always will be.

APPENDIX

THE *FRANKENSTEIN* FAMILY TREE

'You might change the name, but you can't change the brand. That's indelible.'

Lionel Atwill, *Son of Frankenstein*

This look at the many sequels/remakes/variations of the original 1931 *Frankenstein* explores just part of its ongoing legacy – which according to some estimates runs to 400 or so titles. The brand continues to be strong meat.

BRIDE OF FRANKENSTEIN

1935, directed by James Whale. I talk about this film in Chapter Three, but it is worth re-emphasising that the marvelous prologue is like the cult of *Frankenstein* truly beginning. Whale's style is more fluid here than in the original, and the rich comic-dramatic tone is one of the most original approaches of any 1930s movie. Much of what people think of the Monster probably comes from this movie: his groaning utterances ('Friend…good') – made over the doubts of Karloff, who felt the Monster should remain wordless – and his tender encounter with the blind hermit. Yet the dominant figure, in every way, is not the Monster or Frankenstein but Dr. Septimus Pretorius, the fey scientist played by Whale's old friend Ernest Thesiger (who had previously played Horace Femm in Whale's *The Old Dark House*). Elsa Lanchester plays both Mary Shelley and the bride of the Monster, a delicious touch that she explained to *Frankenstein* chronicler Gregory Mank: 'James' feeling was that very pretty, sweet people, both men and women, had very wicked insides....So, James wanted the same actress for both parts to show that the bride of Frankenstein did, after all, come out of sweet Mary Shelley's soul' (1981: 55). Lanchester's Bride is on screen for a couple of minutes, yet such is the force of the image – the scarred face with the cloud of shock-waved hair – that she permanently entered the horror canon.

SON OF FRANKENSTEIN

1939, directed by Rowland V. Lee. It lacks the personality of the previous two pictures, but Universal's handsomely-mounted *Son of Frankenstein* is a remarkably fine studio production. Basil Rathbone plays a junior Frankenstein as though born to the family, and Karloff makes his final bow as the Monster. Here the *Frankenstein* mythology is fully engaged: there is much mention of the abnormal brain, the famous experiments of the past, and a heavy emphasis on scientific talk of electricity and blood. The film comments on the *Frankenstein* phenomenon, as Rathbone's character complains that the family name is 'synonymous with horror, monsters. Why, nine out of ten people call that misshapen creature of my father's experiments – ' at which point his lament is capped by a train conductor shouting 'Frankenstein!' It is also a reminder that the Universal monsters owe much of their fame to their specificity; Bela Lugosi's Ygor, for instance, is a luridly-imagined marvel of yak fur, twisted spine and Hungarian hissing.

THE GHOST OF FRANKENSTEIN

1942, directed by Erle C. Kenton. A distinct drop-off. This is where Universal relegated the franchise to B-picture status; the movie teems with recycled actors and sets from the previous outings. The Monster is lost to a sulphur pit at the end of *Son*, but (as ever) manages to revive – played here by Universal's new monster actor, Lon Chaney, Jr., with Bela Lugosi returning as the (also mysteriously re-animated) Ygor. Another son of Frankenstein, played by gloomy Cedric Hardwicke, messes about with the usual experiments. This one shows how obsessed the Universal cycle is with its own mythology, even if the details are frequently altered; along with much talk of the previous experiments, there is a flashback to the 1931 original.

FRANKENSTEIN MEETS THE WOLF MAN

1943, directed by Roy William Neill. Universal's monsters collide in the first of the 'monster rallies', with Chaney's Wolf Man dominating the early part and the Monster (Lugosi, at long last) helping bring the house down at the end. Lugosi's Monster originally had dialogue, which was eliminated after the result was deemed laughable; still, the sheer fact of the Universal universe folding in on itself – the indelible Dracula now encased in the equally indelible Frankenstein monster makeup – is head-spinning. Writer Curt Siodmak, who all but invented the werewolf picture with *The Wolf Man*, coins some new *Frankenstein* mythology here, including the idea that the Monster can live a hundred lifetimes (thus retroactively explaining his powers of resurrection at the beginning of each new sequel).

HOUSE OF FRANKENSTEIN

1944, directed by Erle C. Kenton. The dark magic of the word 'Frankenstein' is confirmed by this all-star meeting of Universal's monsters; its presence in a title assures a certain level of box-office interest, and it can co-opt the name of the town where much of the action takes place. Boris Karloff returns to the series, but as a conniving doctor (the Monster is played by Glenn Strange) intent on following in Frankenstein's footsteps. The first act is devoted mostly to Count Dracula, but the Monster and the Wolf Man are thawed out in time for a rousing finale.

HOUSE OF DRACULA

1945, directed by Erle C. Kenton. Another gathering of the clan, with the Monster reduced to extremely limited mayhem – although he is acknowledged to have 'the strength of a hundred men'. At this point in the series, the characters, including anonymous townspeople, speak as though they have seen the previous instalments in the saga, and have a familiarity with monster lore. As much as the shrinking budgets, it was perhaps the self-consciousness of the Universal monster films that made them seem played out – and spoofery would be next.

ABBOTT AND COSTELLO MEET FRANKENSTEIN

1948, directed by Charles Barton. Bud Abbott and Lou Costello inaugurated a new cycle of comedies with this horror hootenanny, which maintains Universal's monster cosmos (Chaney and Lugosi are on board), albeit tongue-in-cheek. Because of its child-friendly mode, this is the first monster movie for many horror cultists. In making the Monster (Glenn Strange again) accessible to even younger audiences, this film paved the way for the commercialisation of his image in everything from breakfast cereal to action figures.

TALES OF TOMORROW: FRANKENSTEIN

1952, directed by Don Medford. A half-hour TV version of the story, with future 'One Step Beyond' host John Newland as the scientist, and a bald Lon Chaney, Jr. as the stumbling Monster. A persistent rumour holds that Chaney was so drunk he thought the broadcast was a rehearsal; however much of that is true, he certainly appears out of it.

THE CURSE OF FRANKENSTEIN

1957, directed by Terence Fisher. Hammer Films' first *Frankenstein* entry, discussed in Chapter Three. In these films, the 'Upstairs, Downstairs' world consists of drawing-room and laboratory, a split personality that veers from polite, well-dressed sets to gory violence. Nothing captures the essence of the Hammer *Frankenstein*s quite like the shot of Peter Cushing sawing off a head from a body, with the operation discreetly occurring just below the bottom of the frame. Hammer's Dracula, Christopher Lee, makes his only appearance as the Monster.

I WAS A TEENAGE FRANKENSTEIN

1957, directed by Herbert L. Strock. The *Frankenstein* tradition for a very specific target audience: teenagers. A great-grandson of the original scientist – played by inoffensive Whit Bissell, perhaps the least threatening actor ever cast in the role – gathers body parts from various dead teens, throwing away the leftovers to a crocodile living in his basement. The placement of such gothic touches within a resolutely subur-ban 1950s world is just one of the film's dislocating effects.

FRANKENSTEIN 1970

1958, directed by Howard W. Koch. Boris Karloff returns, this time as an elderly member of the Frankenstein family, tor-mented by the Nazis during World War II. As the last member of the dynasty, he owns the family estate where a film crew wants to shoot a new *Frankenstein* movie. After a rather good beginning, the promise of this 'meta' approach never really pays off, although the ease of the man who played the Monster inhabiting the role of scientist is interesting to watch.

FRANKENSTEIN'S DAUGHTER

1958, directed by Richard L. Cunha. Another descendant (Donald Murphy) is creating mischief, slipping an experi-mental tonic to teenage Sandra Knight. The Z-movie view of Eisenhower America is intriguing: lots of indicators of youth-culture cred, and when the miserable assistant tells 'Dr. Frank' (like many newcomers to the US, the Frankenstein inheritor altered his name) that his ancestors never used a female brain in their experiments, the doctor replies, 'We're now aware that the female brain is conditioned to a man's world, and therefore takes orders.'

TALES OF FRANKENSTEIN

1958, directed by Curt Siodmak. An interesting relic of a project that never got off the ground: Hammer Films was set to produce a TV series called 'Tales of Frankenstein', but didn't get much past this half-hour pilot, a standard account of creator (Anton Diffring), lab experiment, and unruly Monster.

THE REVENGE OF FRANKENSTEIN

1958, directed by Terence Fisher. Although Peter Cushing's Baron Frankenstein was marched off to the guillotine at the end of *The Curse of Frankenstein*, this film re-instates the Universal tradition of finding miraculous loopholes for its narratives – thus, he returns in this first Hammer sequel, disguised as Dr. Stein and relocated to a German town. As developed over six movies, the Cushing version of the role is the nastiest and most cold-blooded Frankenstein, which makes the Monster (normal looking in his first reanimated form here) even more of a lost, exploited soul. At a crucial moment the Baron's brain itself is transplanted into the Monster, uniting the two characters in a more direct way than ever.

THE EVIL OF FRANKENSTEIN

1964, directed by Freddie Francis. A bizarre entry in the Hammer series, this one feels as patched-together as the Monster (who resembles a papier-mâché *piñata* here – the Monster's looks kept changing in the Hammers, a distinct policy switch from Universal's unmistakable iconography). *Evil* blends a ragged collection of plot elements with a new, distinctively 1960s look – not just in the haircuts and the attitudes, but even in the framing of shots.

FRANKENSTEIN CONQUERS THE WORLD

1965, directed by Ishirô Honda. A demonstration of the flexibility of the *Frankenstein* idea: this is a boilerplate Japanese monster movie (complete with giant reptilian foe for the Monster), adapted for the F-legend. As with most versions, there is a rationale – however insane – for the re-emergence of Frankenstein's Monster; in this case, the heart of the

Monster was brought from one Axis power, Germany, to another, Japan, in 1945. When the atom bomb drops on the science lab, the resulting radiation grows a new Monster from around the tissue.

FRANKENSTEIN MEETS THE SPACEMONSTER

1965, directed by Robert Gaffney. There is no *Frankenstein* template in this ragtag cheapie, just sci-fi tropes about space travel and cyborgs, a great deal of stock footage, and a random Frankenstein reference. At this point, invoking the Frankenstein name was a marketing device – something that would insure the immortality of the character.

JESSE JAMES MEETS FRANKENSTEIN'S DAUGHTER

1966, directed by William Beaudine. This deranged genre crossover puts Dr. Frankenstein's conniving granddaughter out West, where she seizes upon the strongman sidekick of outlaw Jesse James for her experiments. Much duller than its campy title would promise, except for the rainbow headgear required for the Monster, whose post-op name is Igor (some of Kenneth Strickfaden's original gizmos from the 1931 *Frankenstein* are in the lab). Released on a double-bill with *Billy the Kid versus Dracula*.

FRANKENSTEIN CREATED WOMAN

1967, directed by Terence Fisher. It fits the era that Baron Frankenstein (Cushing) would have a Playboy centerfold (Susan Denberg) to work on. Martin Scorsese claims it as his favorite Hammer because the film isolates the human soul; Frankenstein is testing how the spirit can survive cryogenic freezing, and whether this means he can capture a soul. It is the most intriguing Hammer *Frankenstein*, not least for the strange idea – again, suited to the increasingly androgynous 1960s? – that a man's brain could be transplanted into his own girlfriend's body.

FRANKENSTEIN MUST BE DESTROYED

1969, directed by Terence Fisher. A worthwhile Hammer outing, mainly for the pitiful Monster portrayed by Freddie Jones, who in one sequence slumps home to his wife only to find himself unrecognised. Cushing's deftness as Frankenstein was tested in a hastily-added (over the objections of Cushing and Terence Fisher) scene in which the Baron rapes the female lead, an act that makes this scientist the most villainous on record.

MAD MONSTER PARTY?

1969, directed by Jules Bass. One of the oddest offshoots of the *Frankenstein* school, a stop-motion puppet animation from the Rankin-Bass company. Karloff is around to give voice to yet another Frankenstein family member, and the kid-oriented tone of the thing has made it a fond TV memory for a generation of viewers.

ASSIGNMENT TERROR (AKA DRACULA VS. FRANKENSTEIN)

1970, directed by Tullio Demichelli. An abysmal example of European co-production horror (in this case, Spanish and West German money), with a fairly liberal use of the Universal *Frankenstein* makeup and yet another story of various monsters thrown together. Michael Rennie (his last film) plays an alien who revives the classic monsters – including a Monster who resembles a younger, lounge-singer version of Karloff.

DRACULA VS. FRANKENSTEIN

1971, directed by Al Adamson. Bargain-basement production with some aged monster movie actors lending cred: J. Carrol Naish (the hunchback in *House of Frankenstein*), who plays the film's equivalent of Dr. Frankenstein, Angelo Rossitto (the dwarf actor with a long career including *Freaks*), and Lon Chaney, Jr., making his final film appearance, and looking like he is ready to go. The results are risible, fascinating only as an illustration of how the horror tropes can be transplanted into a crazily inappropriate genre (the film began as a biker flick).

HORROR OF FRANKENSTEIN

1970, directed by Jimmy Sangster. An attempt by Hammer to start over on their *Frankenstein*s without Peter Cushing, as younger, smirkier Ralph Bates presents a scientist for the era: amoral, sarcastic, predicting *A Clockwork Orange* (1971). Sometimes dismissed as glib, the movie is actually kept aloft by its sneering tone – but falls down badly with its Monster (David Prowse), a brute who kills as soon as he gets the chance. The film does have the highest cleavage ratio of any Hammer *Frankenstein* picture, no easy victory.

LADY FRANKENSTEIN

1971, directed by Mel Welles, Aureliano Luppi. A spirited attempt at Euro-horror, with the requisite washed-up Hollywood star (Joseph Cotten), reigning sex symbol (Rosalba Neri, billed here as Sarah Bay), and plenty of atmospheric sets. Within the zany story can be read a feminist overthrow of the traditional storyline; Frankenstein's daughter calculatedly learns the details of re-animation, then seduces her father's assistant into agreeing to donate his brilliant brain to the body of a hunky handyman.

BLACKENSTEIN

1973, directed by William A. Levey. An eruption of the 'blaxploitation' movement, this utterly incompetent film nevertheless shows the elasticity of the *Frankenstein* model as it engages race and the Vietnam disaster: here the mad scientist uses a Vietnam vet amputee as the subject of his experiments.

FRANKENSTEIN

1973, directed by Glenn Jordan. A made-for television version of the story, shot on video by the team that produced the gothic soap opera *Dark Shadows* (led by producer/co-writer Dan Curtis). Hampered by a pedestrian script and the very limited production style, this one nevertheless tries to return to the Shelley novel, with a particular emphasis on the sympathetic nature of the Monster – known as 'The Giant' here, and ably played by Bo Svenson.

FRANKENSTEIN: THE TRUE STORY

1973, directed by Jack Smight. A second full-scale TV version from 1973, this one a classier affair, although the script by Isherwood and Bachardy departs considerably from Shelley's original. A strong sense of the tragic imbues this dramatically uneven effort, with a couple of age-of-Aquarius innovations, including the fact that the Monster (Michael Sarrazin) begins his new life as a beautiful creature and only gradually begins to disintegrate.

FLESH FOR FRANKENSTEIN

1973, directed by Warhol *protégé* Paul Morrissey. Released in the US as *Andy Warhol's Frankenstein*, the 3-D film's campy outrageousness puts Morrissey's genre-warping talents vividly on display. Gory and hilarious, the film is utterly of the 1970s – postmodern, trashy, cheekily gay.

FRANKENSTEIN AND THE MONSTER FROM HELL

1974, directed by Terence Fisher. The final bow for the Hammer series, and an intriguing one: Peter Cushing's Baron has installed himself as experimenter-in-chief at an insane asylum, where acolyte Shane Briant comes to assist. The Monster (David Prowse) may be the most hideous of the Hammer run, yet blessed with an intelligent brain; the shot of the hairy beast picking up a violin is one of the most plangent in the *Frankenstein* oeuvre. The savage ending is all the more disturbing because of this.

YOUNG FRANKENSTEIN

1974, directed by Mel Brooks. Equal parts affection and parody, Brooks's (and co-writer/star Gene Wilder's) glorious send-up of the Universal originals is just right, down to the last detail – hump jokes and all. An important ingredient of parody is the assumption that the audience will be familiar enough with the original to appreciate the jokes; in the case of the *Frankenstein* films, this was a given in 1974.

THE ROCKY HORROR PICTURE SHOW

1975, directed by Jim Sharman. The cult film par excellence springs directly from *Frankenstein*, but as a fever dream: a rock musical in which a 'sweet transvestite from transsexual Transylvania' named Frank N. Furter creates a new man in his lab – all played for put-on horror-comedy. The film's success as a midnight-movie landmark somewhat obscures how really sharp it is as a genre send-up (and as a musical). The sequel, *Shock Treatment* (1981), also hatched by composer/co-star Richard O'Brien, flopped.

FRANKENSTEIN ISLAND

1981, directed by Jerry Warren. Of all the cheap grindhouse titles utilising the Frankenstein brand, this might be the worst: a nonsensical story about a reanimation experiment on an island populated by leopard-skin bikini-wearing women, with the added horror of John Carradine – once a stalwart of the Universal horror pictures – appearing as the disembodied head of Dr. Frankenstein.

FRANKENWEENIE

1984, directed by Tim Burton. Half-hour film made before Burton became famous, about a little boy named Victor Frankenstein who brings his dog back to life. This is an example of a 'monster kid', using the imagery he grew up on. (See below for Burton's expanded 2012 version.)

THE BRIDE

1985, directed by Franc Roddam. A promising idea – a youth-tinged take on *Bride of Frankenstein*, with a rock star (Sting) and Jennifer Beals, the *ingénue* from *Flashdance* – but the movie is not half as interesting as that. As is so often the case, the real interest is in the Monster and his struggle, embodied here by the looming, sensitive Clancy Brown.

GOTHIC

1986, directed by Ken Russell. The whimsical prologue of *Bride of Frankenstein* expands to provide the fodder for three closely-grouped films, of which this overbearing melodrama is the first. It's the summer of 1816, and Mary Godwin's nightmare lights up the Villa Diodati. Here the Frankenstein myth folds easily into the auteur picture – this is every inch a Ken Russell movie, complete with fire and brimstone.

HAUNTED SUMMER

1988, directed by Ivan Passer. The second Villa Diodati picture, a sort of summer-of-love version with Lord Byron puffing on opium and free love the order of the day. Alice Krige makes perhaps the most intelligent, mysterious Mary Godwin yet seen on screen.

FRANKENSTEIN UNBOUND

1990, directed by Roger Corman. A sci-fi variation that folds together the Byron-Shelley literary group with a real-life Dr. Frankenstein, a strong concept that also includes a time-travel element. It does not entirely stitch together, but the ideas are more scintillating than the previous Shelley-centric pictures.

MARY SHELLEY'S FRANKENSTEIN

1994, directed by Kenneth Branagh. After years of low-budget exploitation, *Frankenstein* got a top-shelf production – only to run afoul of an overheated approach and puzzling casting (Robert De Niro is a mumbling Monster). In its wrongheaded way, this film captures its *zeitgeist*; it is a gassy, over-dressed Hollywood multiplex picture.

GODS AND MONSTERS

1998, directed by Bill Condon. Speculating on the final days of James Whale (Ian McKellen), this film ingeniously uses the imagery of his *Frankenstein* pictures to conjure up Whale's personal demons – and to suggest the value of dark metaphor in spectators' lives.

VAN HELSING

2004, directed by Stephen Sommers. A stupefying 'monster rally' gathering the various Universal heavies, with *Dracula*'s vampire-hunter (Hugh Jackman) the heroic lead. Although a leaden exercise in special effects, the film's most functional element is its depressed, tortured Monster.

FRANKENSTEINS BLOODY NIGHTMARE

2006, directed by John R. Hand. An ultra-low-budget, frankly experimental effort starring the Florida-based director, ranging from genuinely eerie to exasperating (the latter including the title's missing apostrophe). If Mary Shelley's template can absorb this, it can absorb anything.

THE FRANKENSTEIN SYNDROME

2010, directed by Sean Tretta. This bargain-basement effort is poorly executed yet full of ambitious ideas: an illegal lab doing stem-cell research, human trafficking, re-animation with Christlike side effects. Originally *The Prometheus Project*, a title that is an inexplicably arty miscalculation in the history of Frankenstein-related exploitation.

FRANKENWEENIE

2012, directed by Tim Burton. The director adapted his 1984 short for this animated black-and-white 3-D extravaganza; the main story still revolves around a pet dog summoned back to life, but includes many more creatures large and small. It ends in a gratifying monster apocalypse visited on the hero's small town.

HOTEL TRANSYLVANIA

2012, directed by Genndy Tartakovsky. From Adam Sandler's production company, a crass but fast-moving monster rally in Dracula's hotel. Sandler voices Dracula, who has problems with his daughter; the Frankenstein Monster (Kevin James) is sensitive about teasing and still afraid of fire. The movie far outgrossed *Frankenweenie*.

THE FRANKENSTEIN THEORY

2013, directed by Andrew Weiner. A Frankenstein story for the found-footage subgenre, as a documentary crew follows the descendant of the real-life model for Shelley's novel into the Arctic. Not scary, but a clever working-out of the old myth with new technology.

BIBLIOGRAPHY

ARTICLES

Associated Press (2008) 'Frankenstein burger creating buzz in Sikeston' (23 August).

Bordwell, David (2007) 'The Adolescent Window', *David Bordwell's Website on Cinema* (17 November).

Churchill, Douglas W. (1935) 'Hollywood's Weekly Contribution', *New York Times* (3 February) p. X4.

Crisler, B.R. (1936) 'The Monster, Incognito', *New York Times* (9 February) p. X5.

Eisenberg, Arlene and Howard Eisenberg, with Boris Karloff (1962) 'Memoirs of a Monster', *The Saturday Evening Post* (3 November).

Filmograph (1931) (April 25) (accessed via *The Lugosi Scrapbook* website).

Gibbs, Wolcott (1932) 'Dr. Frankenstein and Mr. Sweeney', *The New Yorker* (27 February).

Gleason, Alfred R. (1931) 'Frankenstein', *Variety* (12 December).

Hall, Chapin (1932) 'Various Happenings in Hollywood', *New York Times* (14 February), p. X4.

Hall, Mordaunt (1931) 'A Man-Made Monster in Grand Guignol Film Story', *New York Times* (December 5), p. 21.

Jameson, Richard T. (undated) 'The Night of the Hunter', University of Washington film series program note.

Karloff, Boris (1957) 'My Life as a Monster', *Films and Filming* (November).

Mank, Gregory J. (1985) 'Mae Clarke Remembers James Whale', *Films in Review* (May).

McCabe, Joseph (2012) 'Exclusive: Guillermo Del Toro Talks

Frankenstein, Hulk and More!', *Shock Till You Drop* (October 3).

Morris, Gary (1993) 'Sexual Subversion: The Bride of Frankenstein', *Bright Lights Film Journal* (Issue 11).

_____ (1998) 'Queer Horror – Decoding Universal's Monsters', *Bright Lights Film Journal* (December).

The New York Times (1931a) 'A Young Producer and His Plans' (14 June), p. X4.

_____ (1931b) 'Projection Jottings' (30 August), p. X5.

_____ (1931c) 'Frankenstein Finished' (11 October), p. X5.

_____ (1931d) 'Clive of 'Frankenstein' (15 November) p. X6.

_____ (1931e) 'James Whale and Frankenstein' (20 December), p. X4.

_____ (1931f) Advertisement for 'Frankenstein Incorporated,' p. BR12.

_____ (1935) 'Ogre of the Make-Up Box' (31 March).

_____ (1936a) 'Vampires, Monsters, Horrors!' (1 March).

_____ (1936b) 'A Chat with Laemmle Jr.' (3 April) p. X6.

_____ (1938) 'Revival of the Undead' (16 October) p. 160.

_____ (1939) 'Oh, You Beautiful Monster' (29 January) p. X4.

The New Yorker (1941) 'Cinnamon and Old Toast' (1 February) p. 10–11.

Nugent, Frank S. (1935) 'The Bride of Frankenstein', *New York Times* (11 May).

Papamichael, Stella (2007) 'Walk the Line: 2-Disc Edition DVD', bbc.co.uk (16 August).

Sennwald, Andre (1936) 'Gory, Gory, Hallelujah', *New York Times* (12 January) p. X5.

Sisk, Richard (2008) ''Maverick' John McCain has come a long way since Vietnam', *New York Daily News* (31 August).

Tunley, Roul (1958) 'TV's Midnight Madness', *The Saturday Evening Post* (16 August).

BOOKS

Currell, Susan and Christina Cogdell (eds) (2006) *Popular Eugenics: National Efficiency and American Mass Culture in the 1930s*. Athens: Ohio University Press.

Curtis, James (1998) *James Whale: A New World of Gods and Monsters*. Boston: Faber and Faber.

DeFalco, Tom (2003) *The Hulk: The Incredible Guide*. London: DK Publishing.

Dick, Bernard F. (1997) *City of Dreams: The Making and Remaking of Universal Pictures.* Lexington: University Press of Kentucky.

Drinkwater, John (1931) *The Life and Adventures of Carl Laemmle.* New York: G.P. Putnam's Sons.

Fitzgerald, F. Scott (1986) 'Crazy Sunday', *The Stories of F. Scott Fitzgerald.* New York: Scribner Classic/Collier.

Freud, Sigmund (2005) *The Uncanny.* London: Penguin Classics.

Gatiss, Mark (1995) *James Whale: A Biography.* London: Cassell.

Gifford, Denis (1973) *A Pictorial History of Horror Films.* London: Hamlyn.

Greene, Graham (1993) *The Graham Greene Film Reader*, edited by David Parkinson. London: Carcanet Press.

Hearn, Marcus and Barnes, Alan (1997; rev. edn. 2007) *Hammer: The Hammer Story.* London: Titan Books.

Hitchcock, Susan Tyler (2007) *Frankenstein: A Cultural History.* New York: W.W. Norton.

Jensen, Paul M. (1996) *The Men Who Made the Monsters.* New York: Twayne Publisher.

Johnson, Tom (1997) *Censored Screams: The British Ban on Hollywood Horror in the Thirties.* Jefferson: McFarland.

Jones, Stephen (1995) *The Frankenstein Scrapbook.* New York: Carol Publishing Group.

King, Stephen (1981) *Danse Macabre.* Secaucus: Berkley Publishing Group.

Lindsay, Cynthia (1975) *Dear Boris: The Life of William Henry Pratt A.K.A. Boris Karloff.* New York: Alfred A. Knopf.

Mank, Gregory William (1981) *It's Alive! The Classic Cinema Saga of Frankenstein.* San Diego: A.S. Barnes.

McGee, Mark Thomas (2001) *Beyond Ballyhoo: Motion Picture Promotions and Gimmicks.* Jefferson: McFarland.

Milano, Roy et al.(eds) (2006) *Monsters: A Celebration of the Classics from Universal Studios.* New York: Del Rey.

Schatz, Thomas (1988) *The Genius of the System: Hollywood Film-making in the Studio Era.* New York: Pantheon.

Shelley, Mary (1981) *Frankenstein.* New York: Bantam.

Skal, David J. (1993) *The Monster Show: A Cultural History of Horror.* New York: Penguin.

Vieira, Mark A. (2003) *Hollywood Horror: From Gothic to Cosmic.* New York: Harry N. Abrams.

Weaver, Tom, John Brunas and Michael Brunas (2007) *Universal Horrors*. Jefferson: McFarland.

Wood, Robin (1979) 'An Introduction to the American Horror Film', *The American Nightmare: Essays on the Horror Film*, ed. Robin Wood and Richard Lippe. Toronto: Festival of Festivals.

INDEX

Abbott and Costello Meet Frankenstein 36, 100

abnormal brain 3, 9, 17, 52–5, 60, 98

All Quiet on the Western Front 18, 66–7

Arsenic and Old Lace 36

Atwill, Lionel 10, 97

Aurora monster models 7, 41

Balderston, John L. 16–17

Bissell, Whit 39, 101

Blackenstein 18, 55

Boles, John 58–9, 61, 70

Bordwell, David 10–11

Boyle, Danny 85

Branagh, Kenneth 90, 110

Bride of Frankenstein 6, 11–12, 20, 27–8, 30–1, 49, 51, 55, 62, 82–3, 89–90, 93, 96–7, 109–10

Bride, The 90, 109

Brooks, Mel 4, 43, 55, 62, 84–5, 108

Browning, Tod 28, 35, 77

Burton, Tim 90–1, 109, 112

Byron, Lord 14, 30, 89, 110

Cabinet of Dr. Caligari, The 20, 60, 78

Carradine, John 10, 109

Cash, Johnny 86

censorship 24–5, 46, 72

Chaney, Lon 28, 87

Chaney, Lon, Jr. 8, 10, 34–5, 87, 99–101, 106

Clarke, Mae 18, 58–9, 61, 70, 74, 79

class 61, 76

Clive, Colin 18, 20–4, 45, 49, 51, 54, 58, 69, 70, 72–4, 82

Coleridge, Samuel Taylor 48–9

Condon, Bill 89, 111

Cooper, Alice 88

Corman, Roger 9, 89, 110

Curse of Frankenstein, The 39–40, 87, 101–2

Cushing, Peter 10, 39–40, 101, 103–6, 108

De Niro, Robert 90, 110

Deane, Hamilton 16

deformity and disfigurement 16, 55, 65

del Toro, Guillermo 95
Dracula 10, 16, 18, 20, 24–6, 28, 32–34, 60, 68, 77
Dr. Jekyll and Mr. Hyde 28, 95

Edeson, Arthur 58, 67, 77
Eisenstein, Sergei 60
eugenics 40, 53, 55
Evil of Frankenstein 103

Fairey, Shepard 94–5
Famous Monsters of Filmland 38
Faragoh, Francis 17
Fisher, Terence 39, 101, 103–5, 108
Fitzgerald, F. Scott 20, 75
Flesh for Frankenstein 42, 108
Florey, Robert 16-17, 28
Fort, Garrett 17
Franken Berry cereal 42
Frankenstein (1910) 16, 44
Frankenstein (1973 TV film) 107
Frankenstein (2011 play) 85
Frankenstein 1970 39, 102
Frankensteinia 52, 92
Frankenstein and the Monster from Hell 107
Frankenstein Conquers the World 9, 42, 103
Frankenstein Created Woman 55, 104
Frankenstein Island 109
Frankenstein Meets the Wolf Man 34, 66, 99
Frankenstein Must Be Destroyed 105
Frankenstein, or, The Modern Prometheus 15

Frankenstein: The True Story 42, 95
Frankenstein's Daughter 102
Frankenweenie (1984) 90, 109
Frankenweenie (2012) 91, 112
Freaks 25, 28, 47, 55, 106
Freud, Sigmund 56
Frye, Dwight 10, 18, 21, 49, 68, 70
Fuseli, Henry 79

Gifford, Denis 6
Ghost of Frankenstein, The 34, 99
Gods and Monsters 89–90, 111
Gothic 89, 110
Greene, Graham 30–1

Hammer Films 9, 39, 87, 101–2
Haunted Summer 89, 110
Horror of Frankenstein 106
House of Dracula 35, 55, 100
House of Frankenstein 34–5, 55, 91, 100, 106
Huston, John 17, 23, 85

I Was a Teenage Frankenstein 9, 38, 40, 75, 101
Invisible Man, The 29

Jesse James Meets Frankenstein's Daughter 41, 104
Johansen, David 88
Journey's End 17–18

Karloff, Boris 8–10, 13–14, 18–22, 28–32, 34–6, 39, 41, 45, 54, 63–6, 79, 81, 86–8, 97, 98, 100, 102, 105

Kerr, Frederick 18, 23, 56, 76

Laemmle, Carl 2–3, 20, 66
Laemmle, Carl, Jr. 16, 18, 23,
    66–8
Lanchester, Elsa 20, 41, 98
Laughton, Charles 28, 41
Lee, Christopher 39–40, 101
Leni, Paul 20, 67
Lewis, David 18
Lugosi, Bela 2, 10, 16–18, 28,
    34–6, 66, 87, 98–100

Mad Monster Party? 105
Man Who Laughs, The 13, 20
Mary Shelley's Frankenstein 90,
    110
McCain, John 85
McKellen, Ian 90, 111
Melford, George 16
'Monster Mash' 88
Monster Squad, The 86
Morrissey, Paul 42, 108
Munsters, The 4, 42
Murders in the Rue Morgue 17, 28

Naish, J. Carrol 106
Night of the Hunter, The 41
'Nightmare Theatre' 2, 6, 8, 11

Old Dark House, The 28–9, 41,
    61, 98
O'Brien, Richard 43, 109

PEZ dispensers 87
Pickett, Bobby "Boris" 88
Pictorial History of Horror Movies,
    A 6
Pierce, Jack 9, 13–15, 19, 30,
    41–2, 65

Polidori, John 14
Prowse, David 106, 108
Psycho 93

Rathbone, Basil 34, 55, 98
Revenge of Frankenstein, The
    55, 103
re-release of Frankenstein 33–4
Rime of the Ancient Mariner 48
Rocky Horror Picture Show, The
    43, 108
Roger Corman's Frankenstein
    Unbound 89, 110,
Russell, John 17
Russell, Ken 42, 89, 110

Sangster, Jimmy 39, 106
Scarface 46
Shelley, Mary Wollstonecraft
    Godwin 5–6, 15, 17, 20,
    27, 30–1, 35, 38–40, 42, 44,
    47–8, 52–3, 56, 62, 71, 79, 81,
    85, 87–9, 92, 95–6, 98, 107,
    110–12
Shelley, Percy 14, 30, 89, 110
Sherriff, R. C. 17
'Shock!' TV collection 37–8, 86
    Son of Frankenstein 34, 55,
    97–8
Sorrows of Young Werther, The
    62
Spirit of the Beehive, The 84–5
Strange, Glenn 34–5, 100
Strickfaden, Kenneth 21, 43,
    67, 104

Terminator, The 86
Thesiger, Ernest 62, 98
Tommy 42
Towey, Joe 2

Universal Pictures 5–6, 8–10, 13, 15–16, 18, 20, 22–3, 26–7, 29–30, 32, 34–7, 39, 42–3, 46–7, 61, 66–8, 80, 83, 86, 88, 90, 92, 95, 98–100, 103, 105, 108–9, 110

Van Helsing 91, 111
Van Sloan, Edward 3, 5, 10, 18, 23, 46–7, 50, 59, 69–70
Veidt, Conrad 13
Villa Diodati 14, 30, 89, 110

Warhol, Andy 42, 108
Waterloo Bridge 18, 61
Webling, Peggy 16–17
Wells, H. G. 28, 30

Whale, James 13, 17–22, 24–5, 27–30, 34, 36, 40–1, 46–53, 57–63, 65–7, 70, 73, 75–82, 89–90, 95, 97–8, 111
Wilder, Gene 43, 108
Winter, Edgar 88
Wolf Man 4, 8, 34, 36, 88, 99–100
Wolf Man, The 34, 99
Wood, Robin 57, 61
World War I 17, 20, 72

Young Frankenstein 4, 43, 55, 62, 108
Young Frankenstein (stage musical) 85

Zucco, George 10